Jenny Lind

Sang Here

NORTH STAR BOOKS

Jenny Lind
Sang Here

BERNARDINE KIELTY

Illustrated by Douglas Gorsline

1 9 5 9

HOUGHTON MIFFLIN COMPANY BOSTON

The Riverside Press Cambridge

Also by

BERNARDINE KIELTY

Marie Antoinette

The Fall of Constantinople

Once upon a time there was a plain, unwanted little girl named Jenny Lind who lived in poverty in Sweden. One day as Jenny sat at the open window singing to her white cat, the maid of a dancer at the Royal Opera House of Stockholm walked by, then stopped in astonishment to listen. Rushing to her mistress, this maid gave a glowing account of the lovely voice she had heard. And so Jenny was "discovered," was given singing lessons, and in time became not only the darling of Stockholm, but of all Europe and finally America as well.

The Queen of Sweden gave Jenny a beautiful watch which would always tell her when it was time to come home to Sweden.

The enthralled King of Denmark gave her a little golden shoe.

The Queen of England gave her a jeweled nightingale.

And the whole world gave her its heart.

And so the Ugly Duckling became a swan, as in the fairy story her friend Hans Christian Andersen wrote about her.

In Jenny Lind Sang Here, *Bernardine Kielty has written the true story of the Swedish Nightingale — the career, the loves, the heartbreaks, and the triumphs of a great woman and a great singer. Turning these pages one may sometimes hear an echo of that pure voice still ringing down the years.*

STERLING NORTH

General Editor

CONTENTS

Jenny Lind

Sang Here

Welcome!

I

It was the first Sunday of September, a beautiful summer day in 1850.

The morning sun shone on thousands of people gathered along the waterfront of New York City, from the tip end of the island at Battery Park up the river to the big dock at Canal Street. The crowd was thickest around the dock, pushing and shoving for a point of vantage. At the south end the watchers, with an unbroken view, shaded their eyes as they gazed eagerly out across the shimmering water toward the harbor entrance.

The harbor was alive with boats. Schooners tied to the docks along the river, rocked gently with the tide, their decks covered with people. Steamboats whistled shrilly as they came over from Staten Island, up from Rockaway, across from New Jersey, down the Hudson, bringing more numbers to swell the crowd. Young men were rowing small boats, shouting at one another, tipping dangerously in the waves of larger vessels. Horns were blowing, flags were flying. For the steamship *Atlantic*, bringing Jenny Lind from Europe, was due to arrive at noon.

New York had been turning out since before daylight. Dressed in their best Sunday clothes the people were now beginning to show signs of wear, even though their excitement was growing tenser by the minute. Families had come in groups. But soon fathers began to wander off, gathering with other men in knots, talking loudly, laughing, leaving their wives to hold the brood together. They were workmen, free for the day, tradesmen, pleased with themselves — everybody friendly with everybody else. Here and there a thin shifty-eyed lad slipped through the dense crowd, always on the move, watchful. Mothers held their children's hands tighter when they saw such a one, and men quickly felt their pockets for their purses.

The crowd continued to pour in. Horse-drawn omnibuses filled to overflowing swerved around the corner from Varick into Canal Street, the horses foaming from the extra weight and the extra speed. Even before they stopped, passengers who had been hanging on to the doors jumped off and ran toward the waterside.

All kinds were out today — except the very top layer. And in New York in 1850, the social top layer was very thin. A few coachmen in carriages drove down Broadway and across Canal, moving as close as possible to the edge of the crowd to let their people alight; then wheeled about and drove back eastward searching for a spot for their vehicles so that they too could get a look. They tethered the horses, unloosed their checkreins, and in some cases, where the coachmen looked forward to a good long wait, slipped on a nosebag of feed.

It was a magnificent day, and 30,000 people were enjoying it to the hilt.

Jenny Lind was the most popular person in the world in 1850, and she was coming to our shores. She may have been the best known public figure ever to set foot in America. Already the beloved of Sweden, Denmark, Germany, Austria, England, she was the toast of the great capitals of the world — Vienna, London, Berlin, and Copenhagen. She was said to be a greater favorite with the English even than their own young Queen, Victoria herself. The palaces of kings were open to Jenny Lind. Queens, duchesses, countesses threw bouquets at her feet. The common people followed her carriage through the streets of whatever city she visited. Even the peasants in the fields, who could not read or write, had heard of her.

This was not an overnight popularity. Jenny Lind hadn't flown the Atlantic, like Lindbergh, or swum the English Channel, or led an army into battle. She hadn't married a prince or been a movie star — because there were no moving pictures, and there would be none until many years after she and all those who worshiped her were long dead and buried. Jenny Lind was a singer, as most of the world still knows, even though she lived a hundred years ago. Her name has been handed down to children, grandchildren, great- and great-great-grandchildren. Her picture can still be found in old family albums — such was her lasting fame. She sang with the purity and naturalness and trills and lightheartedness of a bird. All over Europe, and now in America, they called her the Swedish Nightingale.

But Jenny was something more than a great singer. . . .

JENNY LIND'S LIFE was a fairy tale come true.

Even nature seemed to take a hand. On the night of October 6, 1820, in the sky over the city of Stockholm, capital of Sweden, the Aurora Borealis burst forth in a spectacular array of many colors. It quivered and gleamed and flashed in one of the most brilliant displays of the northern lights that the people of Stockholm could remember.

On that night a little girl was born to poor parents on a back street. She was an unwanted baby. Her mother, Anne-Marie, was twenty-seven years old, her life had been hard, and she was a harsh, embittered woman. Niclas Jonas Lind, the child's father, was younger, gayer, and more easygoing than his wife. He was too easygoing, in fact, and it was Mrs. Lind who had to work to support the little family. She did this by running a dayschool for girls in her own small house, where a baby would be only a nuisance. There was an older daughter, Amalia, who was gentle and sweet. The mother loved Amalia, but not the new one, whom she called Jenny.

When the baby was only a few weeks old, Anne-Marie put her out to nurse. She sent her to a little village named Sollentuna, about fifteen miles north of Stockholm, to be taken care of by the wife of the church organist. Sollentuna was in the country, which was a matter of more significance than the hardhearted Mrs. Lind would ever have planned. Although Jenny Lind lived there only as a little child, the countryside left its mark upon her. And also music. As the organist practiced daily in the church close by his house, the majestic chords of the organ, the simple melodies of hymns, the magnificence of Bach, must have sounded and resounded in her ears. So that even in those four earliest years, the broad foundation stones of her later taste were laid. Love of nature and love of music were firmly implanted in her infant memories.

But this idyllic existence ended all too soon. When Jenny was four her mother took her back home, and then began the really black years of her unhappiness. If good taste and natural joyousness had been nurtured in the little girl's spirit in Sollentuna, the seeds of self-distrust that never left her were planted at this time by her own mother.

It was a dingy house on a narrow street that she went back to, with not enough light and air, and not enough nourishment, with no love, and no laughter.

Anne-Marie was always poor, her husband was a ne'er-do-well, her pupils paid very little. She was mother, teacher, houseworker, always surrounded by children, always nervous, and constantly distracted. She was cross, and the weight of her ill-temper fell most often on Jenny.

But Jenny was not without spirit. In Sollentuna she had chatted and sung and run about freely, and naturally she continued to do the same at home — until her "noisiness" further frayed her mother's nerves.

Once her thin singsong stopped suddenly, and a loud slap resounded.

"Oh, Mother!" cried Amalia, and the other girls cowered behind her as Jenny's face reddened under her mother's blow.

Interference only annoyed Anne-Marie. She could not let out her ill-humor on paying pupils, she loved Amalia too much to mistreat her, so Jenny continued to be the scapegoat.

Although only four, she had to go to school classes with the others. Since she naturally could not keep up with them, she was punished as a dunce. The most frequent punishment, because it was the easiest way to get Jenny out from under foot, was to stand her in a corner with her back to the room. There she stood, with her yellow hair hanging straight, and her black apron strings tied behind her back.

Soon the girls would hear a plaintive little call: "Come here and I will kiss you!" This was Jenny's way of saying that now she would be "good" — that she was sorry for whatever it was that she had done.

She was not a pretty child. Her hair was too yellow, her skin too sallow, her nose perhaps a little too thick. But there was an endearing wistfulness in her expression, born of this childhood unhappiness, that remained in her eyes to the end of her days. All the natural joyfulness of little girlhood drained out of her during those years in her mother's school, and the lack of affection made her crave it above all else. Throughout her life, deep down in her soul, she longed above everything for a real home, for love, for protection.

Jenny's grandmother, Fru Tengmark, was indirectly her savior. "Mark you!" the old lady told her daughter Anne-Marie. "That little girl will bring you fame one day!"

But Anne-Marie shrugged her shoulders impatiently.

One day a troop of soldiers headed by a military band marched past the house, and as they marched, played an elaborate and lengthy fanfare of trumpets. Shortly after they had passed, Fru Tengmark heard the thin sound of the old square piano in the next room. It was a piano Anne-Marie had bought for Amalia to play scales on. From its tinkling keys she

now heard the exact notes of the long fanfare which the band had played. She opened the door quietly. But not before the child on the stool heard her. In a flash she slipped off and hid under the piano, fearful of being punished. (In later years Jenny Lind told her own children about this incident. She even played the fanfare, so well had she remembered it.)

Fru Tengmark was a deeply religious woman, and her strict beliefs left another indelible mark on little Jenny, who in her own time became also very strictly religious.

For a time Jenny lived with her grandmother at the Home for Widows, which was pure joy to the child. She liked to sit with her grandmother. She had enough to eat. No one pestered her and she could play all day long with the white cat that also lived there.

The white cat with its blue ribbon! She never forgot it.

One summer day when Jenny was nine, she was sitting in the open window singing to the cat. It was a simple everyday tune but, in the way she had, Jenny added little frills and trills.

A young woman, passing by, heard her and paused to listen. What a flow of beautiful sound! She listened through the whole song and could not put it out of her mind.

As it happened, this young woman was the maid of a dancer at the Royal Opera House of Stockholm. When she got home she gave her mistress such a glowing account of the extraordinary child's voice she had heard that the dancer sent for Jenny to come to see her.

This was the beginning of the fairy story.

Mrs. Lind, grumbling, but with a sharp eye for some possible chance to make a little money, took Jenny to the Royal Opera House to see the dancer, who listened to her sing. "Here is genius!" she cried. There was no question in the dancer's mind.

The child must be trained for the stage, she told Mrs. Lind. But Mrs. Lind, and also Fru Tengmark, it must be admitted, were scandalized. The stage! These two women, in their narrow-minded way, considered the theater a den of corruption and immorality. However, as the prospect of money-payment loomed larger, Mrs. Lind ungraciously gave in.

The dancer at once sent Jenny, with her mother, to the singing master of the Royal Theater. Mrs. Lind went with dragging step. Even on the stairs of the theater, holding her child by the hand, she nearly turned around and went home. Should she let this daughter of hers add to the frivolity of a sinful world? But her feet, beside her daughter's small ones, continued up the steps. "Money . . . Money," went her thoughts, keeping time.

When Herr Croelius, the teacher, heard Jenny sing, he too was overjoyed.

Jenny was only nine, shy, awkward, still broadnosed and yellow-haired. But the path of her life had come to an abrupt turn. The supreme head of the Royal Theater, Count Puke, said first that he could not be bothered with children, especially—he probably added to himself — with an unattractive child. But when he heard her sing he was strangely moved. This was indeed genius!

From singing to the cat in the window, to the stage

of the Royal Theater!

The Count drew up a contract which Mrs. Lind — under protest — signed. She was "sacrificing" her child, but the child was going to be taught by the best singing teacher in Sweden, with all her expenses paid.

Again — at the Theater School — Jenny became the youngest student. But there were no heartbreaks here. She worked hard, for young as she was she seemed to understand how important it was. She not only learned to sing, but to move with a grace that never left her. In later years audiences were particularly struck with her beautiful gliding walk. She learned poise and dignity, and became a lovely dancer.

The school was housed in a fine old eighteenth century building in the heart of the city. To leave its broad halls, as she had to every night, and go back to the grimness of the Lind home was a nightmare. It was a double life she led, industrious, happy, and appreciated on the one hand, threatened and scolded on the other. But the spirit of the school prevailed.

Her eighteenth year was the turning point. On March 7, 1838, Jenny Lind made her debut as prima donna in the Royal Opera. She was to sing Agatha in Weber's *Der Freischütz*. She had already acted in many small parts. Now she was a star. This was the pinnacle.

Pale and frightened, the slender young girl stood be-

fore the audience for her great aria in the second act. She had everything to win or lose. The white spots that were faces below her, stretched on and on, up and up in the enormous black void of the opera house . . . silent . . . waiting.

Then, in one and the same palpitating moment, the strains of the orchestra echoed within her. She felt the presence of Herr Croelius in the wings, she caught her cue, and her lovely lilting voice rose in song. It soared in triumphant sound . . .

The applause was like thunder, with endless curtain calls, and bouquets thrown from the boxes. Young Jenny Lind was a stupendous success!

"I got up that morning one creature, and I went to bed another," she told her friends, and, many years later, her own children. "I had found my vocation!" All the rest of her life she celebrated March 7 as her second birthday.

The unloved child, born in poverty on a Stockholm street, had become the darling of the city.

3

AT EIGHTEEN Jenny Lind was on top of the world. All the great houses of Stockholm opened their doors wide to her. If Jenny accepted an invitation the evening was a success. Hostesses sent little notes to her at the theater, other singers began to grow jealous — a healthy sign! — and young men began to take notice.

Her new teacher, Herr Berg, was always her escort, and when she entered a drawing-room on his arm after one of her stage performances, the guests would quickly pass the word: "Jenny Lind," "Jenny Lind is here."

Jenny stepped lightly on clouds of glory. She was slender, still pale. But she did her hair a new way — in ringlets that hung down over her ears — and always wore simple white dresses. It emphasized her air of youth and purity. Her large deep blue eyes, in spite of the gaiety of her walk and the delight in her smile, were still a little sad. They gave the faraway, out-of-the-world look which people never forgot. She was already a "personality."

Jenny loved parties — under Herr Berg's protection. She sparkled as she greeted her admirers. She was grace itself as she glided across the wide rooms. When she danced her feet scarcely touched the floor. Her curls bobbed, her long wide skirts whirled, as she circled in the arms of a smart young officer, or another singer, or a staid father of a family. She was young, popular, and on the threshold of success. She was as much at ease with the great as she was with her teachers and fellow students and stagehands, and the tradesmen whose stores she visited. For a girl who had just emerged from the shadows of a dark home, these were the Elysian Fields.

For two years she led a joyous existence. Never again would she be so completely without a care. She was independent. She received a salary. She had left her miserable home behind her. When she sang, the Opera House was filled. When she was not in the cast the opera sagged. She was everywhere in demand. Her voice soared in passion, and softened delicately in lyrical passages. It trilled and warbled like a bird.

Two young men sang with her who in their separate ways were later to play important parts in Jenny's personal life. One was the gentle young tenor Julius Günther, whose voice melted with hers in opera's love duets. The other was a rich-voiced lively baritone, the Italian Giovanni Battista Belletti.

She was the darling of the university students. Had there been "pin-up" girls in those days, Jenny Lind would have been the favorite. Once she sang in the college town of Uppsala, 2000 attended the concert, and when it was over the students ran beside her carriage singing. They surrounded the house where she was spending the night, serenaded her, and refused to go home without another glimpse of her. The next day an Uppsala newspaper called her "the Nightingale," a name that the whole world took up later.

In 1840 the Swedish Court made her its official singer.

A brilliant career stretched out ahead of Jenny. But

the price was too high. After one of her concerts that spring a well-known critic ventured to ask: *What has happened to the Voice?*

Here and there others began to comment. They noticed a touch of hoarseness where all had been pure and clear before. Jenny herself was aware that something was wrong. Sometimes the note she wanted would not come. Sometimes the tone was bad.

Jenny was genuinely alarmed as time went on and her voice did not improve. *What to do? Should she change her way of singing?* But her Swedish teachers admitted that they had no more to teach her. *Must she take lessons elsewhere? Go away from her beloved Stockholm? Must she lose her hard-earned freedom and return to her grim family? Was she a Cinderella who had had her Ball, and must now go back to rags and poverty?*

At twenty the Nightingale voice was already worn.

The person who came to her aid was Giovanni Belletti, the baritone, who had studied in Paris with Manuel García, at that time the greatest singing teacher in the world. Belletti showed Jenny what scientific singing could do, what singing in the grand Italian manner meant. She must go to Paris, he urged, and study with García!

Jenny was sick with dread. But all her friends, much as they wanted to keep her near them, joined Belletti in urging her to go away. She belonged to mankind, they told her, not to Sweden. "They pushed me out!" she used to say in later years.

Never did a decision take greater courage. To face the world alone in a strange country! But Jenny was proving herself to be a girl of character and determination. Everything was at stake, and she was prepared to sacrifice all her personal inclinations.

In order to raise enough money for the journey to Paris, Jenny made a concert tour of Sweden in the spring. It was a long hard trip, with the wheels of the carriage in which she traveled up to the hubs in mud. She did raise the money. But it was a final indignity to her beautiful voice, which was now further worn by overuse and fatigue.

She sang her final concert in a small crowded church in Stockholm. One of the songs she sang was a farewell written by a Swedish composer who was a dear friend. Tears mingled with the applause.

4

WITHOUT TAKING any time to rest, Jenny left for Paris. She was tired and frightened and sick at heart. The night before setting forth, she wrote letters until dawn. She could not sleep.

The journey, which today might take three hours, took Jenny more than a week. By steamboat she went from Sweden to Lübeck, in Germany; and from Lübeck to Hamburg; by another steamboat from Hamburg to Le Havre, in France; and from Le Havre to Paris by stagecoach, which on the Continent in those days was called a "diligence."

All the world that Jenny knew remained behind her. What lay immediately ahead she could not guess. Had she guessed, would she ever have left Sweden?

Paris was a city of frivolity, a city of feminine graces and freedom of thought. It was still the day of the "salon," where the intellectuals and the fashionables gathered for conversation and discussion — for gossip and ideas. It was the day of famous women — Madame Récamier, the cool beauty whose portrait, reclining on a divan, has come down to us; of Rachel (*Rah-shell*), one of the great actresses of all time; of the fragile Violetta, the living heroine of Dumas' *The Lady of the Camellias* and of Verdi's opera *La Traviata*, who was to die six years later of tuberculosis.

Into this city of spectacular personages, in late spring, came the little girl from the north. Queen Desideria of Sweden, who cherished Jenny, had given her a note of introduction to the Duchess de Dalmatie, a lady of fashion, who at once invited Jenny Lind to her home.

Jenny had long since passed the period of childish excitement in stepping out into the world. The first glow had died down and her natural shyness had taken over. Even in Sweden she had always been uneasy in society. She had no small talk, no social "manners." Now, to enter a room full of "foreigners" was like facing tigers in a cage. But she knew she must go, and fortified by her firm determination, she took the plunge.

The home of the duchess was one of those gray stone palaces in the heart of Paris, so plain and unassuming without, and so exquisitely beautiful within. Jenny was led into an oval room, elegant with mirrors, painted ceiling, delicate chairs and tables. It was dotted with gentlemen and ladies in groups. Perfume filled the air, the murmur of voices, tinkling teacups, light laughter.

This was not hearty fun as Jenny had known it in Stockholm — loud laughing, fast dancing. This was bright, light, effervescent.

And there *she* was — the pale angular girl, in plain clothes, with no powder on her cheeks, no color on her lips, with very little knowledge of the French language, and no notion whatsoever of wit and elegance and sophistication. In Stockholm she had been beloved, sought after, and was at home with royalty and the nobility. Here she was nobody.

The hostess advanced graciously to meet her, but the awkward guest was mute. There was little that either could say to each other. The duchess moved easily and gracefully among her guests, coming back to the agonized Jenny from time to time. Finally she remembered that the girl was a singer, and invited her to sing.

This should have been Jenny's release. This was indeed the language she knew. As she moved to the piano the guests waited politely. The light voices were silent. But instead of the pleasure she always felt once she sat down to a piano, she was now overcome with confusion and embarrassment. No song rose to her lips.

She ran her fingers over the keys trying to bring herself back.

At last she sang. But all that came to her memory

was a Swedish country song. And she sang it badly.
To the guests who had never even heard her name, it
was less than an event. The song was by no means
notable, and the voice was below the ordinary. They
applauded thinly, and after a small polite moment, re-
sumed their conversation.

Unfortunately there was one person in that drawing
room who did know the name of Jenny Lind. One of
the listeners in that fashionable gathering was Manuel
García, the famous teacher for whom she had come
to Paris.

This was the first and the last party that Jenny ever
attended in Paris.

But worse than social embarrassment awaited her.
The next day she went to her appointment with Maestro García unaware that he had already formed an
opinion: that the Swedish girl had none of the quali-
ties needed for singing before a cultivated audience,
and that her voice had no possibilities whatsoever.
This was the man to whom Jenny Lind was now prepared to entrust the training of that frail organ on
which hung her entire life's fortune and happiness.

García went through with the interview from a sense
of professional duty. He gave Jenny the regular tests.
He had her sing scales, and then asked her to sing the
big aria from *Lucia*, "Perchè non ho." Jenny knew the
aria thoroughly. Only the year before she had sung

it thirty-nine times. But now she could not finish it; she sat down and cried.

García who was not without feeling, was sorry for her. But before everything else he was a dedicated musician and teacher. He had to be honest even though he broke her heart.

"Mademoiselle Lind," he said quietly when she had stopped crying, *"vous n'avez plus de voix."* He did not say Mademoiselle Lind, you have no voice. He said, you have *no longer* a voice.

It was the toll of a funeral bell.

She was not yet twenty-one years old, and the greatest teacher in the world had declared her singing career finished. For ninety-nine out of a hundred persons, this would have been the end. But for Jenny Lind it was the beginning.

Religion came to her aid. Jenny had long since come to believe that her ability to sing and to make mankind happy was a gift from God; that the transformation of a poor girl in the shabbiest of surroundings into the greatest singer of Sweden, was a miracle; in all humility she believed that the discovery of the magnificence of her voice on that memorable March 7, 1838, was a revelation of her mission in life. She had been given a great responsibility.

Had it not been for this belief in the Divine Hand, Jenny would probably never have had the strength to make the decision which she then made. "What must I do to get my voice back?" she asked García, so low that he scarcely heard her.

He looked in silence at the pale tear-stained face, the deep-set blue eyes. He felt the childish appeal, but also the stern determination. Even though he had no belief in her voice, he was moved.

For six weeks, he told her, she must not sing a note. She must not even *speak* except when absolutely necessary. (This could not hurt her, he probably said to himself, and if she had an iota of a voice left, it would help.) If she obeyed these rules to the letter, she could then return to him. At the end of that period he would hear her again. If then he thought that anything could be done, he would try to help her. (Privately he added that he never expected to see her again.)

This was the lowest point that Jenny Lind's life ever reached. She had been deeply unhappy as a child. She had been lonely as a girl. She had suffered pangs of fear when she realized that her voice was failing her. But this was the bottom.

Throughout the summer Jenny abstained from singing and talking. But she did not sulk. She worked. She studied in her little boardinghouse room on the Left Bank as if indeed she had a voice. If she had a voice and was to sing in the future, she must know Italian, she told herself, because most opera was sung in Italian. She must study French, because French was the universal language of cultivated people over all Europe. She therefore studied Italian and French diligently. She pored over grammar, covered page after page of notebooks with declensions, conjugations of irregular verbs, genders of nouns, lists of exceptions. She studied musical theory. In her enforced silence, like a nun in her solitary cell, she listened to the sounds of the outside world. Her musical memory recorded the street cries of Paris, and years later she could sing every note of some of these calls. Sometimes she went to the theater, because *if* she were to be an opera singer she would have to act. She saw the actress Rachel, and made mental note of how she herself might have interpreted the same parts. She heard great music. Beethoven had been dead only fourteen years, and she was spellbound by his symphonies. She heard Mozart and Haydn and Schubert, much of their music for the first time.

In her boardinghouse room she was miserably, brokenheartedly homesick.

When the period was up, she went back to García.

He was surprised and pleased at the change that his advice had brought about. Her voice was rested. Maybe he could make something of it after all, but he promised nothing. However, he would give her lessons — two lessons a week for the next ten months.

They then would see.

Jenny now had to *un*learn everything she had been taught in Stockholm, and learn to sing anew. Her vocal organs had recovered from their exhaustion because she was still young. Now she had to learn to breathe correctly, she had to be taught how to "produce" her voice, how to blend the high register with the middle and the low registers. She had to sing scales up and down, slowly, with greatest care, for many hours, every day.

"He takes no notice of me apart from my lessons," she wrote of García to her friends back home. "But I am enchanted with him as a teacher."

In the summer of 1842 her lessons were finished. Her voice was better than it had ever been. It had now developed into a full powerful soprano with a range from B below the treble staff to G in the fourth line above it! Over this remarkable instrument she had complete control. She could hold a note so long that it died off almost into infinity, then swelled out in a glowing rich crescendo. (Only singers can appreciate the work and patience that made all this possible. As a problem in clear enunciation she would work on a single word, *zersplittre*, singing it on a high B-flat for hours at a stretch. She sang the chromatic scale daily, over and over. In fact she continued to do so for twenty-five years.)

Fortunately Jenny was blessed with a "natural ear." "She never sings a hairsbreadth out of tune!" her teacher marveled.

She was now able to write home, "García is satisfied!"

García had "made" her voice. She could never repay him for what he had done for her. Without him her voice would slowly have died away. But in her *art* there was something more than García. Without her own hard work and determination, above all without her belief in herself and in her God-given voice, she never would have become a truly great artist.

Although Sweden had nearly wrecked her voice,

Jenny now wanted fiercely to go back home. She was advised to make her debut in Paris. But Paris and France meant only misery. She recalled that first appearance at the duchess's soiree, the agony of those weeks of silence, the utter loneliness. She hated Paris! She could not get out fast enough!

Once back in Stockholm, she cut the last cord that bound her to her parents. There was a law in Sweden then that until a young woman married, she was under the guardianship of her parents. But Jenny got around this through compromise. She bought a small house for her parents which was to be theirs all their lives. (Amalia, her older sister, had died several years before.) It was in Sollentuna, the village where she had been so happy as a tiny child. It was a peaceful quiet country, and once settled there her parents seemed at last to be satisfied. In exchange Jenny asked their permission to have a legal guardian appointed by the courts to be her adviser on matters both personal and professional. This her family consented to. The appointment went to Judge Henric Munthe, who from then on to the end of his life was Jenny's counsel, her friend, her family, her all. She never made a move or took on a new friend, scarcely made out a program, without consulting him, and in turn Judge Munthe gladly advised her on the most minute matters as well as on the great decisions of her life.

She was free at last. She was a finished artist. The world lay open before her. But in spite of it all Jenny was still unsure. Her friends tried to persuade her to sing in Copenhagen, capital of Denmark, and the nearest big city outside Sweden. But she refused to go. She was afraid.

This appalling lack of self-confidence, which probably stemmed from her mother's early distaste for her and the punishments meted out to her through the long years of childhood, stayed with Jenny Lind all her life; it made every new engagement an agony instead of a joy.

"Suppose I should be hissed!" she cried, begging her friends not to insist.

Finally they gave up. Well, if she feels that way, maybe she could not make good, they said, maybe she had better not try it.

That was all Jenny needed. When *others* doubted her, she bristled. It was always to be that way. Admit to her that *possibly* she could *not* carry through a project, and lo! she would sign any contract, no matter how tearfully she had held back at first.

Now she decided in favor of Copenhagen.

When she left, Queen Desideria gave her a charming little watch. "So that you will see when it is time to come back!" said the Queen.

The Copenhagen concert was a tumultuous success.

One big Norwegian officer who was there burst out crying every time Jenny started to sing. (She was often to have that strange effect upon listeners, especially men.) The King of Denmark hung a necklace around her neck with a little golden shoe dangling from it. Hans Christian Andersen, whose life was to be entwined with hers in the years to come, came to hear her. "You laughed, you wept," he said about her concerts. "It did you good, like going to church; you became a better person!"

Above all Jenny discovered that an artist is a bird of passage. He cannot stay on the home territory. He must fly away, and return only to rest.

5

BERLIN FRIGHTENED Jenny Lind far more than Copenhagen.

All the big opera houses in Europe were vying for her, but Meyerbeer, the famous opera composer, who had heard her at García's in Paris and been charmed by her voice, had persuaded her to accept the Berlin offer first.

Jenny did accept, and went to Germany a few weeks early in order to get the feel of a strange country, and to try to accustom herself to it. Meyerbeer at once took her in hand. He introduced her to the Royal family of Prussia, and planned several evenings where she could sing in the houses of cultivated musical families.

One evening they went together to the home of the English Ambassador, the Earl of Westmorland. Meyerbeer had told the Westmorlands about this wondrous voice, and they had invited a brilliant company to hear her. But when an unbelievably plain girl appeared, pale, with Swedish-yellow hair, badly dressed, and awkward, they thought that Meyerbeer was playing a joke on them.

"*Attendez, Madame!*" he whispered, raising a warning finger as Jenny Lind sat down to the piano. "Wait."

When she sang she was completely transformed. She was exalted. "I first saw an ordinary girl," the Westmorland daughter said later. "But when she began to sing her face shone like an angel's!"

In spite of the praise and adulation in these favored houses, Jenny became more frightened each day as her opening approached. Nothing would have pleased her so much as a command to return to Sweden. But her musical career was moving forward as if indeed guided by a Divine Hand. Meyerbeer had set it in motion. And she met the man who beyond any doubt became the greatest influence in her life, both musical and personal. This was Felix Mendelssohn.

Mendelssohn, at the height of his brilliant musical career at this time, was an irresistibly attractive person. His dark Jewish face was alive with interest, its expression changing swiftly with every passing mood, his brown eyes full of fire. He loved fun, and the evening Jenny met him he was doubled over with laughter at a joke he was telling.

When they were introduced he at once congratulated her on her "great talent." Jenny thought he was just paying her a lip compliment, and she did not ordinarily heed compliments. But this time she blushed with pleasure. "Why do you say that?" she asked.

"Well," said Mendelssohn, "all who have heard you are of one opinion only, and that is rare indeed!"

It was not long before he could judge for himself, and Jenny's lovely voice became his special delight. "She is as great an artist as ever lived, and the greatest I have known. Such personality as hers is not born in centuries."

For Jenny it was as if a bright bird had darted out of the heavens, and lighted close beside her.

By the time she opened in the Berlin Opera, Jenny's powerful friends had become a pyramid of strength. She sang Norma and triumphed. The plain girl was again transfigured into an angel of holiness, but this time the miracle took place before a huge audience made up of the common people of musical Berlin as well as the privileged few. A shoemaker, too poor to buy a ticket, got himself a job as a supernumerary, and went on stage as a soldier. Like the old Norwegian officer in Copenhagen, he too burst out crying.

How a girl so pale and so shy could impassion men of all walks of life was ever to remain a mystery. Was it the sadness in her deep-set eyes? Or her complete absence of coquetry and guile? Or the purity of her white unadorned simplicity that made her every man's dream of ideal womanhood? The ladies studied her intently, trying to find her secret, while their men leaned toward Jenny in troubled absorption, lips apart, forgetful of all else.

For two years Jenny lived and sang in Germany, and it was a period of almost unalloyed joy. She sang with Mendelssohn in Leipzig, the musical center of the world. She sang for the King when he entertained Queen Victoria of England and the Prince Consort, and the King of Belgium. Both Mendelssohn and royalty were enchanted.

She sang Amina in *La Sonnambula*, Pamina in *The Magic Flute*, Alice in *Robert le Diable*. She rode a horse in *Martha*, singing as she entered, with Belletti, as an itinerant Italian beside her. She sang Susanna to his

Figaro. She was Norma, and Lucia.

Again Jenny was the darling of the students. At Göttingen, the famous university city, the students gave her a torchlight procession, and on the morning after the concert accompanied her carriage to the next city, eight of the handsomest students riding beside her for four hours.

At Mannheim the students rushed into her hotel room after she had left and tore the sheets of her bed to pieces, for souvenirs. The only catch here was that an Englishman who was staying at the hotel could not understand why his room was full of young men. The room they had demolished was his, not Jenny's. But

in the meantime the students, in blissful ignorance, were parading the streets, each wearing a rosette made of a piece of white sheet.

In Munich when she went to the opera for rehearsal, the orchestra greeted her with a fanfare. She sang Haydn's *Creation* there on Christmas Day, and gave the entire proceeds of the concert to the orchestra men.

Germany was a paradise of music in those days, and among the brightest stars was Jenny Lind — so bright in fact that Liszt, the spectacular pianist and composer, refused to play at any festival where Jenny sang, because the audience gave her its entire attention.

Vienna now beckoned, and Jenny quailed. Austria was a richer, more powerful country than Germany at that time. Leaving Germany would be the same wrench that leaving Sweden had been before. "They have such excellent singers there! I shall lose my whole reputation!" she cried. That same lack of self-confidence, that same stage fright!

She did finally force herself to go to Vienna, but for three days after her arrival she had a raging headache, and her nervousness was almost beyond control. Again she was desperately homesick.

But she did it. She sang, she performed, she made a smashing success. "The good God did not desert me!" she wrote home to Judge Munthe.

After her first performance she had twenty-five curtain calls, and the Queen Mother threw her a wreath of flowers with her own hand — something that had never happened before. When Jenny left the theater, thousands of people were waiting for her. They un-harnessed the horses from her carriage, and a company of cavalry had to be called out to get her safely to her hotel.

Among the musical friends she met in Vienna was the composer Robert Schumann. When she sang his "An den Sonnenschein" he said, "I feel the sun beating down on my back as you sing it."

"Ah, but who made the sun shine?" Jenny asked. She sang two of his songs at sight without an error.

(Clara Schumann, Robert's wife and close friend of Brahms, also became Jenny Lind's friend, until the two women quarreled about Brahms' music. Jenny detested it. After that a coolness grew up between them.)

Only London and England were left to round out Jenny's European triumphs. For some odd reason, possibly a northerner's vague distrust of lighthearted Latins, she classed Italy with France, and would never sing in either country. But London was determined not to be deprived.

When a certain London agent learned that Jenny was preparing to return to Sweden from Vienna, he left London that very evening in his dinner clothes, caught a boat to Calais, and a train to Vienna. He stood in the wings of the theater when Jenny sang her last concert, and followed her to the lobby of her hotel. She had already broken one contract with a London manager because of her overpowering dread of new places, and this manager was not going to let the Nightingale fly away in any other direction. He took her back with him — to Calais, to Dover, to London.

The London of Queen Victoria was dignified and hearty, solid rather than brilliant, and soon became Jenny's favorite city. England hadn't the aristocratic flavor of old Austria, or the musical precociousness of Germany. But it had enormous wealth. This was the day of England's far-flung empire; business firms were making fortunes, and the young Queen sat happily on the throne with her handsome Prince Albert close by.

Moreover, when Jenny reached London, tired and weary, she found Mendelssohn waiting to greet her!

London already knew about Jenny. The first night she was there she went to the theater and attracted more attention than the play. "That's Jenny Lind . . ." went the buzz. Her face appeared on candy boxes, pocket handkerchiefs; her name was given to dolls and dogs and horses; there was a magnificent yellow tulip called the "Jenny Lind," and a Jenny Lind "pub" ("bar" to us) on the outskirts of London.

Jenny settled comfortably into the British scene, as

usual putting off her opening from week to week. She found herself a little house behind a low hedge on the outskirts of the city. There she had a garden, and for the first time heard a real nightingale sing. "To think that a creature so small . . . !"

She sat in her garden and sewed. She loved to sew because in no other way could she so completely forget the pressure of the demanding world. Her stitches were said to be as perfect as her musical notes.

London soon found Jenny in her retreat. Crowds came to stand around the house waiting for her face at a window, or her light step entering a carriage. The world would not leave her alone. One day Hans Andersen, her Danish friend, traveled out from the city in a horse-drawn bus to visit her. That was a bonanza for the crowd. For Jenny forgot them in her eagerness to see an old friend, and rushed out of the house to greet him amid the glad shouts of the multitude.

Again this simple girl became an intimate of the famous.

Queen Victoria was her musical companion as well as her friend. One time she invited Jenny to sing at Buckingham Palace. The artist who was to accompany her was Costa, the conductor. But he was either not in the mood, or not at ease in the piece. At any rate it was all just a wee bit off, and Jenny was uncomfortable. The Queen at once divined the cause. "Wouldn't you like to sing something, Miss Lind, for which you play your own accompaniment?"

She was the perfect hostess. Jenny sat down at the piano, sang some of her own Swedish songs, and the old charm was fully restored.

Chopin, Polish composer and pianist, the delight of Europe, was visiting England and met Jenny there. One evening they sat together at the piano from nine until one in the morning.

She met Florence Nightingale, the famous nurse-to-be of the Crimean War, and later gave a concert which brought a fortune to the Nightingale Fund. Both of these remarkable women were born in the same year.

She rode in Rotten Row beside the great Duke of Wellington, hero of Waterloo. The horse was not Jenny's best friend. "I shy before he does!" she admitted, and Americans later were to roar with laughter to see Jenny try to mount a horse.

Jenny's opening was the biggest event of the season at Her Majesty's Theatre. Every man was in a white kerchief, as was formal dress in that day, every lady in jewels and a sumptuous gown. The mob outside was so great that clothes were torn from persons pushing their way in. Carriages were in complete confusion and well-dressed women (trying to reach the door) were obliged to slip under horses' heads.

People came from all over the British dominions. Foreign princes were there. The whole British royal family. Queen Victoria threw Jenny two bouquets.

Jenny played up and down the British Isles on a golden tour. Tickets sold as high as $100 and $200 apiece. She was now a rich young woman. Every time she had sung on the Continent, the house had been filled to overflowing. Managers throughout all the countries she chose to visit had been willing to pay high fees. Jenny could now name her price.

She was laden with royal gifts. Queen Victoria gave her a nightingale of precious stones to wear in her hair. The bracelets she received were enough to cover both arms from wrist to elbow. But Jenny had no desire for money or jewels; she gave away more money than she saved. In Sweden she had donated large sums to education, especially for young girls of talent who, like herself, were poor. She gave benefits for hospitals in England. In order to help raise a statue to Handel she sang his *Messiah* and gave the proceeds to the Handel Fund.

"A life passed amid divine sounds and *still diviner* deeds!" said Disraeli of her — Queen Victoria's adored Prime Minister, and one of the most elegant gentlemen of England.

Jenny had reached a pinnacle. The good fairy could have given her no greater prosperity, no greater success in her art, no worthier ways of helping mankind. But she was not entirely happy. The applause of the mighty was not enough.

She had to have a space in which to think.

6

JENNY LIND had the world at her feet.

But she did not want the world. She wanted a home, and love, and peace. She wanted devotion, with someone close by her side.

Jenny had never had a home. She had had less companionship than most girls. When other girls were strolling home from school, arm in arm, she was hard at work singing, dancing, acting. When these same schoolgirls were growing up, their sweethearts were boys who lived in the same town, and probably on the same street. Jenny at that age was having a whole university for her sweetheart. Uppsala was hers. Mannheim was hers. Göttingen was hers. The students adored her. But there was no *one* warm hand to close protectively over hers. No eyes looking long into her eyes, to see in their wistful depths his and her future happiness.

Hans Christian Andersen, famous teller of fairy tales was deeply in love with Jenny Lind. Her life and his were so strangely alike that the same kind fairy might have waved her wand that their two paths might cross. Hans Christian, like Jenny, was desperately poor, son of a Danish shoemaker, born in a small town, ill fed, and unschooled (until a man of the outside world — like Jenny's dancer of the Royal Theater — saw talent in him and provided him with an education). Hans Christian's rise to fame was as phenomenal as Jenny's. All Europe knelt at his feet — princes, crowned heads, the nobility, and most of all, the simple people.

When Hans Christian met Jenny in Copenhagen, he first fell in love with her purity and simplicity. He could not see enough of this wondrous angelic creature. He followed her from Denmark to Germany to England. He wound her round his heart. Time after time he asked her to marry him. But unfortunately, good and kind and loving as he was, Hans Christian Andersen was not a fairy prince. He had large heavy features, and enormous hands and feet. What was worse, to cover up his ugliness, he wore conspicuously fashionable clothes that made him only more grotesque.

One time in Copenhagen he overheard two smartly dressed young men: "Look! There goes our orangutan, so famous now abroad!" They were speaking of him.

This was not the prince that Jenny dreamed of. She liked him, and always called him "Brother," and signed her letters, "Your Sister." But she also was unfeeling — quite as much so as the young men in Copenhagen. When Hans Christian had asked her for the tenth time *why* she would not marry him, she silently handed him a mirror.

(At more than one critical moment in her life, Jenny — usually so kind — showed herself strangely insensitive to another's feelings. It was probably due to the lack of manners in the Lind household, where no one ever was taught to hold back an impulse, however harsh. This left Jenny, for all her worldly experience, somewhat uncouth. She was likely to "speak out" at a moment when silence would be kinder. Or to be frankly honest at the expense of another person's humiliation, as in the case of poor Hans Christian.)

Anderson wrote three of his fairy stories around her: "The Ugly Duckling," story of the early struggles which they shared; "The Angel," and "The Nightingale." The nightingale's song was of course Jenny's own beautiful voice, and the golden slipper which the Emperor wanted to hang around the neck of the nightingale, was the little shoe which the King of Denmark himself had hung around Jenny's young white neck.

One Christmas Eve Hans decided to go to Berlin just because Jenny was to be there. He was invited to a gay party at a nobleman's house, but refused the invitation, certain that Jenny would send for him. He had written her that he would be there. But no word came, and the poor man stayed alone in his hotel room, with all Berlin noisy and festive around him.

Jenny was out with other friends that Christmas Eve. Moreover, Felix Mendelssohn had that day sent her a Christmas present — an album of his songs written in his own hand and illustrated by himself. With such a gift before her, how could she think about her "ugly duckling"?

When Andersen called on her the next day and told her how he had waited and waited, she stroked his hand lightly and called him a child. She would make it up to him, she promised. She'd give a special New

Year's Eve party for him alone. And so she did. On New Year's Eve she had a Christmas tree, and tea and cakes, and later a supper. She sang him one of her big arias, and many simple little songs. It was a perfect party for two good friends.

When Hans did not try to play the role of lover, he and Jenny had jolly times together. They met a little later in Weimar. When Jenny stepped out of the stagecoach on her arrival, there stood Hans Christian waiting for her, the snow falling lightly on his heavy overcoat and big hat. They were both entertained at the Weimar Court, and went on little expeditions in the duke's sleigh. They walked and talked and laughed, for Hans Christian loved to be funny, and Jenny made an appreciative audience. But this was only play.

Unfortunately for Hans Christian Andersen, Jenny Lind, as we have seen, had already met Felix Mendelssohn.

Of course no one knows what goes on in the human heart. But looking back, reading old letters which were saved through the years because the writers were famous people, it seems only too obvious that at that time Jenny was in love.

Felix Mendelssohn was a shining light in the musical world when Jenny entered it. He wrote irresistible music, he was a piano virtuoso, every musician in Europe was his friend. Goethe, the great German poet, loved him. Queen Victoria could not see him often enough on his several visits to London. His own concerts were everywhere immensely popular. He was a strikingly handsome and highly cultivated man, ardent, vivid, alive, born into a suave society that was a world apart from the heavier Scandinavians whom Jenny knew and grew up with.

From that moment when they met — it was at the home of a sculptor in Berlin — Jenny Lind and Felix Mendelssohn were fast friends. Their careers brought them together. They met in city after city in Germany, and later in England. Their lives were inextricably intertwined. Jenny sang in public when Mendelssohn conducted, and in private when he played the piano for her. They took excursions together. She came to know him so intimately that she knew what he was going to say before he spoke. And he understood her in the same way. She was gayer with him than with Hans Christian or anyone else, and laughed long and loudly, because Mendelssohn was wittier and more hilariously funny than anyone she had ever known.

Mendelssohn wrote many songs for her, and the soprano part of *Elijah*, his great oratorio, was written for her voice, of which he knew every quiver.

Once they took a trip down the Rhine together from Cologne to Aachen. At the Aachen Festival, which was their objective, Jenny was in highest spirits. She shed her regular white costume for a dress of sky blue like her eyes, with swansdown around the deep low neck, and fresh flowers in her hair. She was more nearly beautiful than ever before. As always when she was with Mendelssohn, she was warm, fresh, lively. That year at Aachen they called it the "Jenny Lind Festival." (Unlike Liszt, Mendelssohn was pleased to have Jenny, not himself, in the limelight.)

Mendelssohn was thirty-five when they met, and Jenny was twenty-four, innocent and vulnerable. She was an open book. The tragedy of it, for Jenny at least, was that Mendelssohn was already happily married, with a beautiful wife and a home and children whom he adored.

If Jenny had lost her heart, which seems very likely, she surely never admitted it even to herself. With her strong power of will and determination she was able to rise to heights of selflessness. Her friendship with Mendelssohn, on the highest plane of lighthearted happiness, became the greatest blessing of her life.

Had Mendelssohn met Jenny before he was married, both their lives *might* have been different. Who knows? The world of music would have been enriched by such a union, for Jenny would have sung better music under Mendelssohn's tutelage. "She sings best the worst music!" he once said, smiling ruefully about

his dear friend's programs. But with Jenny's strict moral code and her strong character, she probably never for a passing moment allowed herself to think of that Might-Have-Been.

This stimulating relationship left its mark. For one thing Mendelssohn started her singing oratorios and the songs of Schubert and Schumann. But also — and this may sound contradictory — under his influence she became more woman than artist. "I am convinced that she would gladly exchange all her triumphs for simple homely happiness," said a friend of both Jenny and Mendelssohn. She had come wholly alive for the first time.

At his last concert in London, Mendelssohn played the Beethoven *Concerto in G.* "There were two ladies present whom I particularly wished to please," he said, "the Queen and Jenny Lind."

Mendelssohn died in 1847, aged thirty-eight, three years after he and Jenny met.

His death was almost more than Jenny could bear. For three months she sang not a single note. It was two years before she could make herself sing one of his songs, and then it was a young German named Otto Goldschmidt, a pupil of Mendelssohn, who finally persuaded her to do so. Through all the troubles and triumphs that lay ahead of her, Mendelssohn's memory remained alive with Jenny Lind for the rest of her life.

JENNY DECIDED never to marry. But she was young and she was lonely. She was bruised by the blow of her best friend's death. If, at that moment, anyone looked deep into her eyes and put out an appealing hand, her own eyes would surely fill with tears and she would clasp it.

This is about what happened. Julius Günther, the tenor with whom she had sung duets so often in opera, had been following Jenny's fortunes with alternating hopes and fears. His dream was that their duet could last forever. That Jenny would be willing — *sometime* — to marry him. *Would she consent?* he asked himself. *Or would she never look in his direction?* He was hopeful when they traveled about Sweden together so happily, and darkly pessimistic when Jenny made her phenomenal success on the Continent, and spiraled so far above him in the artistic heavens.

The year after Mendelssohn's death, Julius and Jenny met again in Sweden. Perhaps it was on the rebound from that tragedy, but when Günther got up his courage again to ask her, Jenny said *Yes, she would marry him!* At last!

They exchanged rings. They were formally engaged. They were happy. When Jenny again left Sweden, she had eyes only for the slim young man standing on the crowded dock gazing sadly after her as her ship pulled out.

But separation is dangerous for lovers. Especially when the tie that binds them is as fragile as the one between Jenny and Julius Günther

Jenny was in a strange mood. First she said she would never marry. And now she was engaged. Her world had gone topsy-turvy.

She had also made up her mind to stop singing opera forever. This was a problem on which she had been pondering a long time. As she became increasingly religious, she began to believe, as her mother and grandmother had preached, that the theater was evil. Opera was only another form of theater, she reasoned, and she must give it up. She would still sing in concerts, for God had granted her the gift of song to uplift people's hearts. But she would not act.

When she wrote Julius of the radical step she was about to take, he as an opera star was scandalized. He wrote back urging her to reconsider. No doubt she answered vehemently. They quarreled by letter across the water, which is far more serious than quarreling by

voice. There is no room for a sudden shift in mood, or softening of glance — only words, forever there, in black and white.

No one will ever know exactly what happened between Günther and Jenny Lind. Günther left instructions that all Jenny's letters to him be burned at his death, and Jenny herself never again spoke of her engagement. "Please refer no more to the matter of G. and me," she wrote to her guardian. "... it disturbs and desolates my whole being..."

Sometime during the period of the Günther quarrel, Jenny met a young English captain named Claudius Harris, tall, handsome, religious-minded as she was herself, but *heavy* of spirit. "What a dull young man!" she said on that occasion. A few months later she said the same thing, far more emphatically. But in between those two exclamations her whole outlook on life and marriage and art had had a serious upheaval. An earthquake shook her out of all her melancholy sadness.

Captain Harris fell madly in love, and Jenny — still in her strange unpredictable mood — could not resist him, so tall, so handsome, so deeply religious! They became engaged.

What Jenny did not become engaged to, however, was Claudius' mother, who at once took all matters concerning the two young people into her own ma-

ternal hands. Mother Harris considered the stage the handiwork of the Devil. Jenny must *certainly* not sing in opera, she said, and she must put the promise in writing. Jenny must not sing on the stage at all. Jenny must put the financial reins firmly into the hands of her husband-to-be (and her husband-to-be's mother). And leave to her husband-to-be (and her husband-to-be's mother) all decisions of a business and professional nature!

Jenny, just coming into her own independence, was decidedly uneasy.

But the final blow was personal. Still in a tender mood, and still, after all, engaged, she offered one evening to sing a group of new songs to Claudius alone. With all her heart in her lovely voice, she sang through to the end, and then looked up for his approval. Claudius was fast asleep, and slightly snoring.

The marriage was to have been on May 14 in England. But on May 16 Jenny appeared alone at a friend's apartment in Paris, pale and shattered, but determined. She had escaped!

She wrote to her guardian. "Come, come to me!" she pleaded. "If you would only come to Paris and be with me a little!" And good Judge Munthe traveled the long journey from Stockholm to Paris to see his Jenny through her fresh crisis.

When Mendelssohn died, Jenny's heart was broken. When she and Günther broke up, her pride was hurt. But her sense of humor saved her in the Claudius affair. The ridiculousness of the whole episode seemed to clear the air. To be sure, she was worn out. She rested for six months without singing a note. She took the grape cure at Merano. She went to Lübeck to be with dear German friends. And she came out of the ordeal sound of body and spirit.

It was after these six months of recuperation that Jenny Lind received a stupendous offer from P. T. Barnum, the great American impresario, to tour the United States. It could not have come at a better time. She was in the pink of health, her voice had never been better, and she knew exactly what she wanted to do with the remainder of her life (so she thought).

Through an Englishman, as his representative, Barnum offered Jenny Lind $1000 each for 150 concerts, all her expenses paid, her trip both ways across the Atlantic Ocean, the best hotel and travel accommodations that America could offer, horses and carriage always at her disposal. Besides this he would bring over her companion, Josephine Ahmansson, and her young cousin-secretary, Max Hjortzberg.

Barnum also wanted a pianist and a tenor of her own choosing. Jenny suggested Julius Benedict, the conductor-composer who had most often accompanied her in England, but instead of a tenor she made a plea for her good friend Giovanni Belletti, the baritone, which was granted her. Barnum would include two servants for herself and a valet for Benedict and Belletti.

This called for a considerable outlay of money for any day and age. In 1850 it was enough for all of them to live on for the rest of their lives.

Jenny wrote to her dear friend, the wife of the sculptor at whose home she had first met Mendelssohn. "Beloved Friend: I have decided to go to America, the terms are so generous. Since I have no greater wish than to make enough money to found schools in Sweden, I cannot help looking upon the journey as an answer to my prayer. I shall be able in one or two years to gain a very large fortune, and after three years I should not need to sing another note — unless I wished to."

8

"BARNUM WILL PUT you in a cage," people told Jenny Lind when they heard about the proposed trip to America. "He'll exhibit you and charge twenty-five-cents admission!" These were her European managers who were jealous because an American had caught the Nightingale — and a circus manager at that!

But Jenny was in no mood to be sidestepped. She had come to a turning point in her life, and Barnum was beckoning her up a golden path.

P. T. Barnum was, in his way, as remarkable a person as Jenny Lind. In fact it was Jenny's fate, in spite of her own plain ways, always to be surrounded by remarkable personalities: highly imaginative, persistent, overdressed Hans Christian Andersen; enthusiastic, laughing, romantic Mendelssohn; even Queen Victoria, who was something of a "character" in her own right, aside from her indomitable position in the world of affairs.

But most flamboyant of all was Barnum.

(When we speak about Barnum we have left for a time the realm of gentle European fairy tale, and entered headlong into the bustling, hustling, rough-and-ready New World. We leave Jenny Lind to prepare for her fabulous journey, and ourselves look closely at the man who made it possible.)

Phineas Taylor Barnum was born a poor boy in Bethel, Connecticut, in 1810. Connecticut in those days was a severe puritanical state best known for its Blue Laws, and life was made as hard as possible for the boys who were born there.

Phineas' father had a farm. But the boy did not like the farm, or farming. He never took to any kind of manual labor, and managed all his life somehow to avoid it. "Lazy," they called him on the farm.

His father also ran a general store, where Phineas worked when he was old enough. There he could not be called lazy. His brain had to tick fast to keep up with the shrewd old Yankees who used to gather on rainy days, and think up mischief. They were practical jokers, and young Barnum had to be on the alert to avoid being the butt of their jokes (and — when the chance came — to play his own jokes on others). In fact practical joking became a Barnum "specialty" in later life.

Phineas also had to keep a sharp eye on the women. These were the good housewives who brought in eggs and butter and beeswax and goose feathers to exchange for groceries. To keep the store solvent, he had to learn to drive a hard bargain. This too was to stand him in good stead throughout his long career.

He always had a head for arithmetic, and one time when he was only ten years old, his teacher boasted that little Phineas could figure out in five minutes how much wood there was in a given load. A neighbor bet that he could not. Therefore, though it was one o'clock in the morning when the argument took place, the teacher, the neighbor and Phineas' own father, roused him. They gave him the dimensions of the load of wood, and in exactly two minutes the child, awakened from a sound sleep, gave them the correct answer. For his future career, this mathematical prowess, especially when concerned with dollars, became his most valuable asset.

Phineas had his first taste of New York when he was twelve, and was hired to help drive a herd of cattle there. It was January, the snow was deep, the roadways were only paths, and the journey was long and hard. But he saw the big city, and it became a beacon.

This was the boy who eventually became America's greatest showman. Remembering the Blue Laws of his youth, he believed that men, women, and children must have relief from gloom. If he, as their "impresario," could amuse them without corrupting them, he felt that he had not lived in vain. From the exhibition of a monkey that could dance, to the highest realms of music, it was all show business to Barnum. That he made large sums of money in the practical application of his amiable theory, he felt, in no way detracted from its virtues.

Barnum's first step toward nation-wide fame was to buy the American Museum. The Museum was in the heart of New York, opposite St. Paul's Church, at the corner of Ann Street and Broadway. It contained a vast collection of curiosities. Unfortunately Barnum was what we now call "broke," or what he, in his mellifluous way, called "at the foot of fortune's ladder."

But he gambled on his ability to make everyone in New York aware of Barnum's American Museum and eager to visit it. And he won.

He had to figure closely. He was married by now and had a family of his own to support. He reckoned that by living frugally he and his wife and two children could exist on $600 a year; but his wife, always his staunchest supporter, said they would manage on $400.

Within a year he had paid for the Museum from his profits. Daily at sunrise he opened the Museum

and urged visitors from out of town to make a tour before breakfast. He had everything to offer, from moral drama to freaks. The fee was twenty-five cents, with children admitted at half price. In one year alone he netted $27,917.

He caught the public by the forelock. As planned, he spread his name, and news of his Museum, throughout the country. No publicity stunt was too complicated. He gloried in the dramatic and the mysterious.

One day a man came into the office begging money for a meal.

"Why don't you work?" said Barnum, and promptly offered him $1.50 a day for what he designated as "light labor."

The man's job was to start out with five ordinary bricks. He was to lay the first brick on the sidewalk at the corner of Ann Street and Broadway (this was close to the Museum); the second, he was to lay directly in front of the Museum; the third, diagonally across the street near the Astor House; the fourth, opposite, in front of St. Paul's. Then, with the fifth brick in his hand he was to walk quickly around, from one brick to the next, exchanging the brick in his hand at every point for the brick on the sidewalk. He must look serious, pay no attention to anyone, and answer no questions. At the end of every hour, by St. Paul's clock, he was to go to the Museum, show a ticket, and enter. He must then walk solemnly through every hall in the building, go out again, and continue laying his bricks as before.

The man was convinced that Barnum was insane. But he did as he was told, and half an hour after he had started placing his bricks a crowd of 500 people was following him. At the end of the first hour, the sidewalks were packed. Each time the man went into the Museum a score of persons would buy tickets and follow him, hoping to find the answer. This went on, hour after hour, until sundown, and continued the next day, and many days thereafter. The police finally had to ask Barnum to put an end to the bricklaying because the crowds were blocking traffic.

How many tickets were sold this way, Barnum never revealed. But he did admit slyly that they more than paid the man's wages.

Among the famous personalities on display in the Museum were two giants, a French giant and an Arabian giant. They were good friends but jealous, and it took very little to arouse them. One day they had a quarrel of such proportions that they decided only a duel could settle it.

"All right," said Barnum. "That's your affair. But remember, you are both working for me. If this duel is fought, the public is entitled to see it. I shall advertise it, it will take place on the stage, and only if, and when, you kill each other will our engagement be at an end."

The giants declined — then laughed and shook hands.

But it was a little man, not the giants, who made Barnum's lasting fame and fortune. Charles S. Stratton was a bright-eyed, perfectly formed child, with light hair and ruddy cheeks, in the best of health, and, when Barnum first saw him at the age of five, only two feet tall. (He grew a little, but not much, in the years that followed.)

Barnum at once engaged him for the Museum and

started on his publicity campaign. "Imported from England, a dwarf, eleven years of age, by name Tom Thumb," read the sign in front of the Museum when Mrs. Stratton, the dwarf's full-sized mother, arrived with her prodigy. She was indignant. Every item wrong! She'd take the child back to Bridgeport on the next stagecoach! But when she found that her tiny son would be earning $7 a week with a bonus of $50 at the end of the year, she decided to co-operate.

Two years later "General Tom Thumb" was the rage of the country, and his salary increased with his fame. Barnum taught him to sing songs and tell jokes, and dressed him as a full-grown man. He toured the country with him, and then decided to take the little fellow to Europe. When the European trip was planned, Barnum advertised: "Last chance to see Tom Thumb!" and the crowds poured into the Museum. Because of stormy weather, the packet-ship for England was a day late in sailing. "A few hours still remain!" the papers said, and thousands more piled in.

Barnum and Tom Thumb went to Europe together, escorted to the ship's dock by New York's Muncipal Brass Band.

For three years they toured Europe, but it so chanced that they never crossed the Nightingale's path.

Barnum was tired. He was thirty-nine years old. He wanted to rest, to see something of his family, and to build a home. When he finally returned to America, heavily laden with profits, he set about spending them by building what turned out to be the most extravagant and probably the most monstrous house in the state of Connecticut. It was a villa called "Iranistan," designed in oriental style and set in a large park.

The mid-nineteenth century, besides being an era of eccentric personages and of inordinately heavy eating, was also a period of questionable taste in architecture and furniture. "Iranistan" had Turkish minarets, Byzantine domes, Moorish tiles. A large fountain played in front, and iron reindeer and elk stalked through the shrubbery. There were stables and conservatories. Furniture was specially built for each room. Marble statues adorned the curved stairway, Chinese landscapes were painted on the walls. Barnum's study was lined with orange satin brocade. There were pier glasses, chandeliers, white and gold ceilings, and a bath-shower of both hot and cold water. People used to say that "Iranistan" was "elegant as a steamboat."

"Iranistan" cost a fortune, but Barnum charged it to advertising, and as such it paid. Which brings us back — at last — to Jenny Lind.

Were it not for "Iranistan," Jenny Lind might

never have come to America. A picture of the villa was engraved on the stationery on which Barnum had written her. Its elegance convinced her — against all other argument — that Barnum was a man of stature and reliability.

When he was at last able to sit back in the completed magnificence of his new home, Barnum had time to think. Though he was thirty-nine, he had not been quiet a minute of his life. And he couldn't keep quiet now. He wanted to branch out in a new direction. He wanted to give depth to his activities. He was tired of being called a "humbug." What Barnum now proposed was to give the people of America some serious, "high-toned" entertainment.

It happened also to be a strategic moment to approach Jenny Lind. He made her an offer that he believed no one could refuse. It was unheard-of munificence, and Jenny, for the first time asking no advice, accepted.

One item was to be a surprise. When the Jenny Lind party arrived on board the S.S. *Atlantic* they found a piano, sent by Barnum for their pleasure on the trip.

Perhaps it should be added that at the very time Barnum was making his offer, a rival proposal came to Jenny Lind from St. Petersburg, Russia. America won.

9

AT NOON SHARP, the *Atlantic* was sighted entering New York harbor. (The *Atlantic* was one of the largest ships of its day, measuring three hundred feet in length — as against the nine hundred eighty-seven feet of today's *Queen Elizabeth*.) Foghorns tooted, flags waved, and all along the waterfront people cheered, even though the ship was scarcely more than a spot on the horizon.

The *Atlantic* had been on the seas for eleven days, and on each of those days an item had appeared in the New York papers about her famous passenger, so swiftly approaching our shores. Since there was no radio or international cable or even telephone, it was not actual news of the voyage that the American public read, but anecdotes, bright little stories, glowing descriptions, sent daily by Barnum to the news-thirsty papers. Jenny Lind's personality, her life story, her musical triumphs, her fabulous generosity, were publicized, read, and talked about. Jenny was already a dazzling figure.

On September 1, the night before the ship's arrival, Barnum slept on Staten Island, to be that much nearer the harbor entrance. And on this fair Sunday, with all the city waiting, he boarded the tender bearing the health inspector.

Miss Jenny Lind was standing beside Captain West. When she saw a stout man climb over the rail carrying a large bunch of flowers, she knew who it must be. His round face was red and his curly hair damp with exertion.

She made her way toward him at once and extended her hand in greeting.

"Mr. Barnum!"

"Miss Lind!"

Although these two had never met, they were not strangers to each other. Letters had sped across the ocean between them.

As they stood at the deckrail talking, the ship proceeded slowly toward the city, and Jenny gazed for the first time on the New World. "Discovered by my countryman, Cristoforo Colombo!" cried Giovanni Belletti, rushing up to Jenny, as though laying the new country at her feet.

The ship went through the Narrows. It passed Governors Island, Ellis Island, and Bedloe's Island; but no Statue of Liberty stood with raised arm to greet them. It would be more than thirty years before that symbol of freedom would lift her lamp over the harbor.

New York was a beautiful sight. There were no skyscrapers, and would be none for many, many years, but church spires shone in the sun, and the brick houses along Whitehall Street were bright with flags and banners. The round hulk of Castle Garden stood offshore, and behind it waved the trees of the Battery.

As they drew nearer, the mass of people began to take on movement and color. They heard a roar from 30,000 throats. The foghorns continued to toot, hats were tossed in the air, handkerchiefs fluttered, and flags waved. Figures on rooftops could be seen jumping up and down precariously.

Canal Street dock was a solid mass of humanity. The police could not hold the people back. Many were trampled under foot, but none fatally, or so it was reported. Nothing marred the jollity of the crowd that happy day.

The ship docked, the gangplank was lowered, a carpet was laid its entire length, and to the delight of all who could see, Miss Jenny Lind walked off the ship on the gallant arm of the Captain. There she was, smiling gravely, in a gray silk dress that caught the sun, a long pale blue coat on her arm, and a bonnet gay with flowers. Her big eyes were blue as the sky, and her fair hair was smooth. To the eager people waiting there so long to greet her, it was as though an angel had alighted among them.

After Barnum had seated Miss Lind in his carriage with her companion, and her secretary, and the two musicians of her entourage, he himself mounted the box and sat beside the driver. For those who could not see Jenny herself, that well-known portly figure on top, smiling broadly and waving his hand, was reassuring. The Nightingale was here at last! It was difficult for the coachman to guide his carriage with its valuable cargo through the dense mob that milled around them.

"But there are no *poor* people in America!" exclaimed Jenny, looking out at the holiday crowd surrounding the carriage. In Europe she would have seen beggars, the diseased, and the disabled. To her eyes, everyone *here* was healthy, happy, and well dressed.

Jenny was tired and overexcited, but she was to have no rest. At five o'clock the whole party sat down to a fourteen-course dinner!

Jenny looked around the table at her friends. She had invited Mr. Barnum to join them, and here he was sitting on her right, with Giovanni Belletti happily on her left. Around the table were Josephine,

her companion, Max, her secretary, and Julius Benedict, the conductor. The Irving House had turned itself inside out to serve a "bang-up" Sunday dinner, including foods Jenny and her party had never heard of — such as sweet corn and yellow squash.

The murmur of the crowd outside was a constant accompaniment to the table talk. Barnum ran to the window from time to time and peeked through the shutters. "Thousands!" he exclaimed with delight. This milling mass of New Yorkers was his own handiwork. He hadn't exactly invited them, but he had created a lure, and he had done nothing to dissuade them from coming. He'd spent six months on this welcome.

At the end of the long meal Jenny stood up, and in the European manner held her wineglass high. "To our good American friend, Mr. Barnum!" she cried.

The others sprang to their feet to join in the toast.

Barnum stood, but without wineglass in hand. "Miss Lind," he said. "I do not think you can ask any other favor on earth which I would not gladly grant; but I am a teetotaler and must beg to be permitted to drink *your* health in a glass of cold water!"

Belletti, the Italian, and Benedict, the German, and the two Swedish young women, had never heard the word "teetotaler," and had scarcely known a single person who did not drink wine with meals as regularly as tea, and far oftener than water. But Jenny admired Barnum's abstinence. It was another form of that austerity which she held in such respect.

Through the open window the happy murmur grew stronger.

"Would you walk out on the balcony and let them see you?" Barnum asked Jenny, hesitantly. But she shook her head. She had known excited crowds before and they frightened her.

It was always to be like this with Jenny Lind and Barnum, he forever wanting to display her to the world, she seeking the shadows. He wanted publicity, she craved peace and quiet, with only her close friends around her. It was the only point of friction in their long and otherwise congenial relationship. Barnum was a businessman, Jenny Lind was a prima donna. But Barnum was the one who always gave in. *The Nightingale must be happy.*

At midnight, strains of music wafted in. As Barnum had known in advance, two hundred members of the New York Musical Fund Society planned to serenade Jenny Lind. He ran with excitement to the window and beckoned to her.

The crowd made way for the musicians and for the three hundred firemen in scarlet woolen shirts who marched close behind them, carrying lighted torches. It was a spectacle that even Jenny could not resist.

She let Barnum lead her through the open window and out to the balcony.

When the crowd saw her at last, after patiently waiting eleven hours, they let out a shout that could have been heard way up in Greenwich Village. "Welcome, Jenny Lind!"

The band played "Yankee Doodle," and everyone sang. Jenny waved her hand and nodded her head in time to the lively music. The soft September air from the harbor cooled her hot cheeks.

It had been a long day. Jenny and Josephine, Belletti, Benedict, and Barnum could hardly keep their eyes open. New York itself was gloriously worn out. In groups, the crowd now straggled home and gradually the city quieted. Only the grunts of a few pigs could be heard as they nosed hungrily about the emptying streets.

NEW YORK was the great metropolis of the New World, with a population of over 500,000 vigorous, lively citizens. They had to be lively to keep up the pace. The city was growing fast. Country folks were moving in. Every ship brought immigrants from Europe. New businesses were starting. There was money to be made.

The Irving House, where Jenny and her friends were staying, stood at the corner of Chambers Street and Broadway, one of the busiest intersections of the city. From the Irving, Broadway ran straight south to the Battery and the harbor, through the heart of wealth and fashion. It was a scene of perpetual motion. Every kind of carriage rolled over its wide cobbles — fashionable phaetons in which lovely ladies were seated, two-wheeled gigs with high-stepping horses driven by men-about-town, slow-moving hand-drawn carts, and always the hackney cabs. To cross Broadway on foot was a supreme adventure. Buses zigzagged in and out at a dangerous pace. Cabdrivers shouted to each other, waving long worn whips, their dusty hats on the back of their heads.

Every now and then a cab horse fell, and the carriages behind pulled up sharp, shaking the occupants out of their seats and frightening their own horses. Men rushed from the sidewalks to try to hold the horses. A crowd gathered, delighted with any free show.

Jenny would have liked to see New York — to stroll down Broadway on Giovanni's arm as she so often had strolled with him on their tours in Sweden. But when he invited her now, she had to shake her head. A conference with Mr. Barnum! Expected visitors!

This was the first day. But she continued to refuse Giovanni throughout the week that followed. More visitors! Crowds gathered in front of the hotel so thick that she could scarcely reach her carriage! No, no! Jenny could not take a walk!

So Giovanni had to be content with Julius Benedict for a companion, and together the two musicians "saw the town."

One street down Broadway from the Irving was the Astor House, focal point of fashion. Here they saw the cream of New York elegance — the large lobby filled with people, the luxurious drawing rooms with their velvet-covered furniture, sofas, mirrors, potted palms, and brightly lighted chandeliers.

Wealthy bankers and businessmen of importance dropped in at the Astor bar from their nearby offices — energetic, aggressive men, with tall hats slightly tilted; light trousers tighter than Europeans were used to, waistlines narrower; and mostly with whiskers worn fashionably below the chin. This was a man's world.

Outside the Astor, the ladies took over. In the late afternoon of a fine day they could be seen strolling along Broadway, looking in the shop windows, their small parasols at a coquettish angle. Their dresses ran to bright colors, and fluttered with tassels and ribbons, quite unlike the sober grays and plain browns most often seen on the streets of European cities. (European ladies wore their finery only indoors.)

"Every one a beauty!" would be Benedict's reaction. Travelers were always struck with the healthy good looks of New York women. And Giovanni, in spite of his loyalty to Jenny, would have to agree.

Along with the ladies, the two musicians also paused to look in the windows. There they saw "Jenny Lind Hats," "Jenny Lind Parasols," "Jenny Lind Fans." There was a "Jenny Lind Tea Kettle" that sang when the water boiled. The city had gone mad over their Jenny!

What most astonished them was the filth on the streets. Everywhere the ditches were piled high with rubbish, with pigs nosing through it.

The Bowery, another long thoroughfare, was the poor man's Broadway, far livelier, particularly at night, and equally crowded. Though Barnum had warned them not to go out in New York at night, Belletti and Benedict tramped the Bowery sidewalks until their legs ached. Here were the smaller cheaper shops, all open, old folks sitting companionably on doorsteps, vendors calling their wares from the middle of the street: "Tomatoes," "Ole clos," "Shoes." A three-piece German band was always somewhere about, playing loudly and badly, surrounded by a circle of enchanted children. And the Oyster Man in front of his stand, slitting the shells expertly for his customers, talked without ceasing.

Again there were pigs with spotted hairy backs

and long legs. According to the Oyster Man, the pigs trotted out every morning to forage, and returned at night, without any prodding from man or child, each to his own little corner. Most of them, he said, lived in Five Points. At the mention of Five Points he shrugged his shoulders.

Five Points was a blot on New York. It was a small crowded area, huddled around the intersection of five narrow crooked streets, not far from the Bowery. Its dilapidated wooden houses were built helter-skelter, one behind the other, making chase difficult and escape easy. This was where "wanted" criminals hid from the law, a rendezvous for pickpockets, thieves, vagabonds, the riffraff of both Europe and America.

Bands of little girls wandered around on their own, dressed in rags, their hair uncombed, unwashed, bodies thin and emaciated. If they were not homeless, they came from homes too foul to stay in. Organized gangs of ruffians could always be rounded up in Five Points. Even the police were afraid to go there singly. In springtime the mud was knee-deep. In winter the cold seeped through the rickety walls. Disease as well as crime prevailed. . . .

This was New York, city of infinite variety.

For a week Giovanni delighted in it, Jenny was carefully guarded from it, and Barnum whipped it into a frenzy of excitement.

LIFE WAS NEVER DULL around Jenny Lind. This plain, unassuming young woman, who wanted nothing so much as peace and quiet, was destined always to be the storm center of excitement, especially throughout her long stay in America.

This, of course, was how Barnum had planned it. On the day in February when he received the letter announcing that Jenny Lind had accepted his offer for a tour in the United States, he at once set to work. By September 1, everybody in the U.S.A. must know of the Swedish Nightingale.

He started with the conductor of his regular train to New York. "Did you know," Barnum asked him, in a voice vibrant with excitement, "that Jenny Lind is coming to America?"

The conductor shoved his cap back on his head. "Jenny Lind. She a dancer?"

It was as Barnum feared. In America *nobody* knew Jenny Lind!

So Barnum sent her picture to all the publications

— the calm placid face, the big eyes, the smooth hair parted in the middle and brought down over the ears, the air of modesty. He circulated her biography in the newspapers — the poverty-stricken little girl and her spectacular triumphs. Most important of all, he made it resoundingly clear that Jenny would give to charity practically all the money she earned from her concerts. Jenny Lind might be a Nightingale to the rest of the world. To Barnum (and soon to all America) she was an Angel.

Not only was New York prepared. By the time Jenny arrived in America, Barnum had stationed twenty-three agents around the country to pave the way for her coming tour, to prepare the red carpet for her welcome.

The American public, for Barnum's purpose, was one vast "middle class." It consisted of workingmen, storekeepers, and schoolteachers; the very poor and the well-enough-off; the new immigrants from Ireland and Germany, and the old settlers from the New England farms (like Barnum himself). These were the people Barnum was out to impress. He wanted Jenny to be known, not only to the so-called "upper class," but to the millions. And he succeeded.

It is true that the upper classes were curious. He had to turn away ladies whose carriages drew up daily in front of the Irving House. *Was she pretty, or was she plain?* They wanted to know. *Why did she wear her hair in such thick pads at the sides of the face?* Some said she had no ears. That's why she wore it so. They must see. They came bearing gifts of flowers and fruits; eyes and ears alert.

It pleased Jenny to have Barnum stand between her and these mincing elegant "ladies." She was always more at home with the poor, to whom she felt she belonged. With the rich and the frivolous she was uneasy.

One day a Swedish carpenter from Brooklyn called at the hotel and sent a message to Miss Jenny Lind. Jenny was pleased to get a note in Swedish, though she did not recognize the man's name. She invited him up, and shook hands warmly. When he told her who he was, she nearly cried with joy. He had lived near her in Stockholm he told her, and they had been playmates as children! Probably no visitor she received while in America made Jenny happier. The next day she took the ferry to Brooklyn, visited the carpenter's wife and children while he was at work, and left a sealed envelope. When the workman returned home that night and opened the envelope, he found in it a check larger than any he had ever seen. This, she wrote, was for his children — a memento of their father's early friendship with Jenny Lind.

The hall chosen for Jenny Lind's first concert was Castle Garden, the old round fort that stood on an island two hundred feet off the Battery.

The great event was scheduled for Wednesday, September 11. On the Saturday and Monday preceding that day Barnum advertised an auction for the sale of tickets. An enormous crowd gathered. On Saturday he sold a thousand tickets for $10,141, the *first* ticket going to a hatmaker named John Genin for $250. It was good business on Genin's part. He put the ticket on display in his shop window, and from that day on his name and shop were famous. Newspapers throughout the country published the story. To wear a Genin hat became a mark of distinction. That one ticket laid the foundation of his fortune.

The first rehearsal was a bleak failure. As frequently happened, Barnum went too far. He invited all the music critics in town, and they in turn invited their friends. Men carrying violin cases claimed to be part of the orchestra and pushed their way in. The mob, milling around the entrance to Castle Garden, was so dense that Jenny could scarcely get to the door. And the crowd inside — for a rehearsal! — was as large as any she had ever faced in a full-fledged European concert.

The Nightingale's blue eyes snapped in anger.

She was annoyed beyond words by the crowded rehearsal. She had heard about the stupendous sale of tickets at the auction; and now she wondered if the "generous contract" with Barnum were not inadequate and unfair. Gone was the day when all decisions were left to friends and advisers. In America there was no Judge Munthe to appeal to. Jenny was on her own, and she was determined to take action.

When Barnum called for her the next morning, he found another gentleman ahead of him. It was Mr. Maunsell Field, one of New York's foremost lawyers.

"We are speaking of my contract, Mr. Barnum," Jenny said directly, her face flushed in embarrassment as well as determination.

Barnum at once sensed trouble. "Miss Lind," he said before Jenny could catch her breath, "I'm glad you bring it up, because I myself wish to make a slight alteration in our agreement." It was almost as if he had foreseen what was coming.

Jenny was taken aback, and even the urbane Mr. Field raised an eyebrow.

"I am convinced," Mr. Barnum continued, "that our enterprise will be much more successful than either of us anticipated." (The daily demonstrations and the auction would have convinced him of this, if his sound business sense had not already done so.) "I wish therefore to add to our contract that you shall receive not only $1000 for each concert, besides all the expenses as we had already agreed upon, but, after taking in $5500 a night for expenses and for my own services, the remainder of the receipts shall be equally divided between us."

Jenny Lind was dumfounded. In her dreams she could not have hoped for such generosity. She forgot Mr. Field completely and put out her hand to grasp Barnum's. "Mr. Barnum!" she cried. "You are a gentleman of honor! I will sing for you as long as you please. I will sing for you in America — in Europe — anywhere!"

This was from the heart. Jenny was limp in her re-

lief that there was going to be no trouble between them. In time the contract would be broken. But for the moment Barnum was her ideal as a manager.

Barnum's round face beamed. He had procured what he well believed to be the greatest single attraction in the world, and he was not going to jeopardize it for a few paltry dollars. He had been figuring for months on the edges of newspapers and the backs of envelopes. There was money enough for all. Even though — as he admitted later — from the day she landed until the day two years and three months later when she left America he never knew a quiet moment. Above everything else, *the Nightingale must be happy!*

The second rehearsal was better. Or it started better. Jenny had just begun her big aria, "Casta Diva," when the building shook with the boom of a cannon. She stopped singing. Then started again. A second gun went off. Then a third. Then a fourth. Finally Jenny burst out laughing.

California had just that day (September 9, 1850) been admitted to the Union as a state, and New York was greeting the news with a hundred-gun salute.

"It must mean good luck," Jenny said. "Just when I come, America reaches from ocean to ocean!"

But Jenny was not so certain of her good luck as the first concert approached. The newspapers had praised her extravagantly. "Her method is fertile; her manner fervid; her execution finished to the last possible degree..." "Tonight will appear a divinity of song..." "Jenny Lind is the most popular woman in the world at this moment..."

All that adulation, all these adjectives, before she had sung a note in public!

"I am frightened of such praise!" cried Jenny. "I am full of imperfections... I shall tremble when I come to sing!" How true her prediction was no one could have guessed.

Castle Garden was not a concert hall, it was an arena. But Barnum was well experienced in handling crowds. To make seating easier in the big ungainly building he had divided it into four sections. Each section was lighted with its own color, red lamps, green lamps, blue lamps, yellow lamps. The tickets for each section were printed in the corresponding color, and the hundred ushers wore rosettes and carried wands of the color of their particular section. In order to prevent confusion, the doors were opened at five o'clock, though the concert was not to start until eight.

Jenny arrived in the middle of the afternoon. She was uneasy, nervous, and her hands were cold. Even Giovanni's words of encouragement did not calm her.

But she was the only one depressed. The city

itself was on tiptoe with excitement.

From the moment the door opened, the audience began to filter in. An awning two hundred feet long covered the bridge that led to the entrance, now flooded with light. Beyond the gate where the carriages pulled up stood a double row of policemen extending a full block. Carriages were allowed to drive to the gate only from the Whitehall side, then pass into Battery Place. "One-way traffic" was having its first New York tryout. People who had no tickets were crowding to see the lucky ones who did have them. Hundreds of boats were anchored close around the old fort, filled with would-be concert listeners. But they were doing their own celebrating, and their fifes and drums drowned out all other sound.

One well-known New Yorker, Nathaniel Parker Willis, told later of strolling down Broadway on his way to the concert. Most of New York was going his way, he said, but he saw some dandies swinging their canes, walking north with their backs to Castle Garden, and a few smart carriages deliberately driving in the opposite direction, as if to show their superiority to "Lindomania."

"They'll soon realize how silly they are!" said Nat Willis to himself. For him Jenny was the Woman of the Generation.

Inside Castle Garden the gaslight shone brightly

from large chandeliers. The flags of Sweden and the United States were floating from the stage, and a large bank of flowers was massed on the balcony. "Welcome Sweet Warbler," it said in asters and roses.

How many there were in the big audience that night varies with the telling. Some say 5000, some 7000. According to Nat Willis, only about one-eighth were women. Their men had probably left them at home lest they be trampled under foot. He counted only eleven persons who belonged to the elite. The people present were real New Yorkers — enterprising folk who always make up the core of a big city crowd, people from all parts of town, from all walks of life, from all degrees of income — the gay, the sentimental, the eager. They were the kind of audience Jenny would have chosen had she been able to do so.

Not only New Yorkers! There was even a Russian in that crowd, a wealthy young Russian, in America on business, and sailing the next day. Above all things he wanted a ticket for this concert of concerts. He was willing to pay almost anything. He tried all the music stores and hotels where tickets had been sold after the auction, but none was left. Finally at five o'clock that day he went down to Castle Garden and mingled with the crowd. He offered a large sum of money for a ticket. But no one was willing to sell.

As in any New York crowd of that day, there were doubtless a few sly characters from the Five Points region slipping their oily way through the carefree mob. At any rate our Russian, who was obviously a man with money to burn, felt a hand creeping into his pocket. He grabbed the hand and held the man in a vice. "I got three children ... a sick wife," whined the pickpocket. But the Russian made him a proposition: if he could pick a pocket with a ticket in it, he'd not only let him go free but he'd make it worth his effort.

Not long afterwards the thief came back with a fat wallet that contained a ticket for the concert.

So our Russian was in the audience.

(The next morning the unhappy man whose wallet had been stolen got it back with a ticket for Jenny Lind's *next* concert, and twenty pounds in cash. "Having offered the sum of twenty pounds unsuccessfully for a seat," said the accompanying note, "I enclose that sum for the use of yours. Hoping you will enjoy the concert of which I so unceremoniously deprived you, believe me, dear sir, your very obliged *Fanatico*.")

Everyone that first night was in his seat in good time. On the dot of eight the orchestra of sixty men filed onto the stage, followed by their conductor Julius Benedict. They were applauded heartily. They played their overture, and the audience listened and again applauded.

Next came the handsome Giovanni Belletti with his velvety baritone voice. He sang nobly, and again the audience clapped, this time even louder, because they were relieved that the period of waiting was almost over. They had eyes and ears only for Jenny, and now the breathtaking moment had arrived.

A hush fell over the enormous gathering. Then Benedict came onto the stage leading Jenny Lind. She said later that she could not have walked on without her hand in his.

She was a vision in white, with a long full-skirted dress that reached to the floor. She seemed to glide, not walk. Her face was not beautiful, but the set of her head on her shoulders was unbelievably lovely, enhanced by the soft deep ruffle that fell away from her low round-necked gown. A few purple pansies had been tucked in the smooth yellow hair drawn over her ears. Her big eyes were blue as the sky, with long dark lashes and that look of faraway sadness which people could not forget. She never wore rouge, and now her face over the footlights was dead white. There was that wistfulness about her, that childlike simplicity and purity such as this audience had never seen. It called up a deep-down, hitherto scarcely suspected want in the heart of the beholder. To all these men, many of them hardheaded, loud-mouthed, shrewd "go-getters," she was the ideal of modest womanhood.

They saw the vision in one full glance. Then the entire audience stood up spontaneously and gave three roaring cheers. Hats were thrown in the air, handkerchiefs waved like a sea before her.

Never before had there been such an ovation, said Barnum later, and this time he did not exaggerate.

But alas for Jenny! The ordeal was almost more than she could bear — this new world, these alarmingly vital people, the lack of any privacy for ten days, the sense of being a puppet on a string strained her nerves to the breaking point! The constant noise, the overeating, the wild rehearsals, above all, the paeans of praise! She was always frightened when she sang in a new city. Now she was numb with fear.

She managed to make a deep curtsy. She made it in true humiliation before these warmhearted admirers. They were expecting so much! And *what could she give them?*

Giovanni and Barnum, standing in the wings, could see her tremble. Her white skirt shook. Her face to the audience was even more deathly pale.

Her opening number was "Casta Diva" from *Norma*, chosen because it showed off to the greatest advantage all the effects of her beautiful voice — all the achievements of her wonderful technique. She had conquered Europe with "Casta Diva." Now she sang her first notes, in America, and they could scarcely be heard.

Barnum's round face grew red.

But once more Jenny's unconquerable will came to her rescue. Almost before the audience could detect what had happened, she recovered. Her voice regained its strength and soared in all its wonted sweetness. It was light, bright, sure. In its softest notes it could be heard by everyone in the hall, no matter how far from the stage. She held a note to the infinite reaches of pianissimo until it had all but died away, and then slowly made a crescendo back to full force. Her face came to life. Her eyes flashed. She sang "Casta Diva" as she had never sung it before.

The concert proceeded to its triumphant climax. When Jenny had sung a duet with Giovanni, when she had sung a trio, her lovely voice accompanied by two flutes, when Benedict had conducted the orchestra in one of his own compositions, then at last Jenny sang the music that this big kindly audience had been waiting for — the simple folk songs from her own country, and a rather dreadful but rapturously applauded "Greeting to America."

This was the end. Applause, shouts, cheers, bouquets flung onto the stage. Everyone radiating happiness.

Jenny smiled now with real pleasure. Her face for the first time was flushed pink. When for tiredness she could not step on stage again, the audience called Barnum.

"My friends," said he, his face wreathed in smiles, "you have often heard it asked, 'Where's Barnum?' Now you may well say, 'Barnum's nowhere!'"

He held a paper in his hand, and said that although Miss Lind had asked him not to mention it this evening, he could not resist telling them of her magnificent generosity. Miss Lind's share of the concert, he told them, would be close to $10,000, all of which she was giving away. And he listed the charities — the "destitute," the "friendless," the "indigent," Protestant, Roman Catholic, the Fire Brigade, the Musical Fund Society!

New York had never had such an evening!

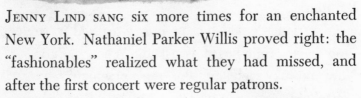

JENNY LIND SANG six more times for an enchanted New York. Nathaniel Parker Willis proved right: the "fashionables" realized what they had missed, and after the first concert were regular patrons.

The Nightingale was a success. But the Angel was besieged.

Barnum had unlocked the dike when he read aloud the fabulous gifts that Jenny Lind was making to the poor of the city. Now the generous lady was surrounded by the greedy and the ill-bred. Well-dressed people called at the hotel on various pretexts and ended up asking for charity.

"Is *that* all!" exclaimed one woman to whom Jenny had given money.

"We've come for a *donation*, not *alms!*" said another.

Jenny could not rid herself of them. "I have given away so much!" she wrote indignantly to her guardian, to whom she made regular financial as well as personal reports. "I must run away from this pack of ravenous wolves!"

She looked forward to Boston as a respite.

Boston in 1850 was charming. Its houses were fresh-looking, with bright red bricks, window and door trims very white, blinds and area railings very green. Brass knobs and doorplates shone with polish. Even the signboards of the streets were freshly painted. Up on the hill overlooking the waving trees of the Common shone the gold dome of the State House. Boston was then the fourth largest city in the United States.

It was a city of imposing men — William Lloyd Garrison and Wendell Phillips, ardent Abolitionists, working for the freedom of slaves; Louis Agassiz, naturalist, then teaching at Harvard; Ralph Waldo Emerson and Nathaniel Hawthorne; poets Longfellow and young James Russell Lowell, with the older John Greenleaf Whittier not far away; statesmen Edward Everett and the mighty Daniel Webster, Senator and orator for New Hampshire.

But in spite of the roster of names, Boston was said to be less pretentious socially and less given to luxurious living than New York.

Jenny wanted to travel there by boat, though there were by now many railroads operating in New England. A boat trip would be more peaceful.

So Jenny thought. But she reckoned without Barnum. "Somehow," word got about. As their vessel, the *Empire State*, steamed through the East River toward Long Island Sound, every institution on every island was out to cheer. As they passed Blackwell's Island, now Welfare Island, there were the prisoners massed on the shore to greet Jenny Lind. (Prisoners always depressed Jenny and she crossed to the other side of the boat to avoid seeing them.) At Ward's Island the immigrants saluted her with shrill fife-and-drum corps. At Randall's the children of the orphan asylum waved their hands and called out "Jenny Lind!"

Moreover, when they reached Boston, going the last part of the way by train, they found an enormous throng surrounding the railroad station waiting patiently in driving rain, under bobbing umbrellas. The coachman who drove Jenny Lind to the Revere House, where she was to stay, assisted her into her carriage, and later offered to let the public kiss the hand that had held Jenny Lind's (for five dollars a kiss).

Jenny's first concert was a brilliant success, and Barnum followed it with a reception to which all the notables came, including the Governor, the Lieutenant Governor, *and* Daniel Webster. With his great domed forehead, his deeply resonant orator's voice, and his courtly manner, he impressed Jenny more than any other American she had met.

Nevertheless, she wanted to escape the crowd, and one day when Giovanni, his dark eyes sparkling, asked her if she would like to drive with him into the country, she clapped her hands. Whether it was for his company or the countryside he didn't dare question. It was enough for him that she would go!

It was a fine autumn day, the trees were bright with color, and once they were outside the city the two escapees hopped out of the carriage and walked hand in hand along the roadside. They had a lovely time. The rocky soil and the oxen pulling carts, the tall men in the fields reminded Jenny of Sweden. She could have run with joy.

Passing a small farmhouse, she saw a woman working in the doorway and stopped to speak to her, motioning Giovanni to walk on. The two women chatted, about children, crops, cooking. The farm woman seldom got to Boston, she said, but two lucky neighbors of hers had tickets to hear the famous Jenny Lind.

"Oh!" she sighed. "To hear the Nightingale!"

Without saying who she was, Jenny started to sing softly. In her beautiful rich voice she sang a song that all her audiences heard. The woman smiled dreamily as she listened.

When they finally said goodbye, Jenny put five dollars into the woman's hand. "Now tell your friends that *you* have heard Jenny Lind!" she said, and ran happily down the steps to join Giovanni.

Another pleasant incident was her visit to Harvard College. The Honorable Edward Everett, former minister to Great Britain and retired president of Harvard, was captivated by Jenny Lind and invited her to Cambridge to see the College. (Harvard had 500 students at that time and Cambridge was a pretty town of white houses and lofty elms.) Mr. Everett took her into the Observatory to look through the telescope at Saturn, in beautiful view at that time. But when Jenny put her eye to the instrument she was nearly blinded by a meteor which at that very moment streaked across the sky — the brightest meteor visible in those parts in nine years the astronomer told her later.

It was a portent, people said, of Jenny's own brilliant progress across America!

Her concerts at Tremont Temple were a delight to the appreciative, sensitive Bostonians.

"She looked as if she stepped down, out of a poem," said the Reverend Peabody.

"She sings like the morning star," said poet Longfellow, "liquid heavenly sounds . . ."

But the music critics, much as they appreciated her

voice, wanted to hear it displayed in music better than Swedish folk songs, and "John Anderson, My Jo" and "Comin' Through the Rye." They wanted to hear her sing good solid German music.

This was what Mendelssohn had always said, deploring the more popular music on which she had actually made her fame. "She sings beautifully such bad music!"

So, to satisfy this more cultivated Boston taste, on Saturday night, October 6, she sang a program of the sacred music of Handel and Haydn. In "I Know That My Redeemer Liveth," from *The Messiah*, she reached heaven. She sang it through two times, and, after the second time, continued to stand before the audience, entranced, her eyes gazing afar, her face glowing with feeling. A halo seemed to circle her fair head. For her and for every person in that hall it was a deep musical and religious experience.

If this had only been the last Boston concert!

But as usual Barnum pushed too hard. He considered Tremont Temple too small. He could sell twice as many seats as the hall held. So he scheduled the last concert for the old Fitchburg Depot, a barn of a place down by the railroad tracks.

All the seats were snapped up at once, after which Barnum began selling standing room ("promenade tickets," as they called them then).

Standees were not supposed to enter the hall until eight o'clock. But they began arriving at six, and by half-past six a thousand were milling around the Depot. No seatholder could possibly push his way through this solid wall. The police could not make a dent in it.

The hall had only two entrances, and each was approached by a narrow stairway. At ten minutes before eight the crowd pushed open the outside doors and made for the stairs. Coats were torn off, ladies fainted but had no room in which to fall.

It was a hot night for October, and when the hall was filled the air was stifling. All the windows were locked tight. "Break 'em!" someone shouted. And as the orchestra started to play the overture, glass crashed and splintered.

Belletti sang. But no one heard him.

When at last it was Jenny's turn, the crowd tried to listen but the noise of the hard-breathing mass of packed humanity drowned out her voice.

Then came another shout: "The floor is going!" Cries of terror mingled with the music. This time the concert had to come to a complete stop until Mr. Benjamin Pierce, America's foremost scientist of that day, stood up on a chair and assured the audience that the floor was of such construction that it could hold their entire weight, and more.

If Barnum had not quietly disappeared, it is hard to say what might have happened to him. He did succeed in returning later, still without being observed, in order to take Jenny back to her hotel.

It was a terrifying experience, and when Barnum peeped into the little room where Jenny and the others were waiting, Jenny looked at him icily.

The next day he swiftly escorted the party out of town, but left an agent to return the money to those indignant ticket holders who never got inside the door.

In an attempt to mollify his prima donna, Barnum now invited her, with Josephine and Giovanni and Julius Benedict, for a brief visit to "Iranistan." Noth-

ing could have been better designed to soothe Jenny's raw nerves. The trees were still a brilliant red and gold, and the air was crystal-clear.

Friendly again, Jenny walked around the garden with her hand on Barnum's arm. The towers and turrets of the oriental villa rose behind them, fountains sparkled, and statues appeared among the bushes. "How can you leave this beautiful place to travel around with me?" Jenny asked.

Barnum smiled. Already he was plotting the tumult and the shouting of their next stop. But he said nothing to disturb her.

When they reached Philadelphia, their next new city, the crowd was so dense that Jenny's carriage

could scarcely move from the dock. "*How* do they *know?*" wailed Jenny. And Barnum's round face was bland and innocent.

The crowd followed her to the hotel. "Jenny Lind-O! Jenny Lind-O! Come to the Wind-ow!" they called.

"Only one glimpse, Miss Lind," Barnum begged.

But Jenny was adamant.

Finally behind Jenny's back, he motioned to Josephine Ahmansson to put on Jenny's bonnet and shawl and appear at the window. Josephine did so and waved her hand. The crowd cheered happily, and soon drifted off. But Jenny never knew why.

The Philadelphia raggle-taggle gypsy crowd was keen about Jenny Lind, but the more select gathering at the Chestnut Street Theatre, who had paid good money for their tickets, were determined not to be carried away. Philadelphia audiences had the reputation of being the most difficult-to-please in the country, and Philadelphia was going to keep its head!

This was the first concert where Jenny faced a coolly critical audience. The customary overwhelming ovation, such as New York and Boston had given her, was missing. *Jenny Lind had to show them*, in Philadelphia!

This reception must have struck a chord of memory. Jenny knew what it was like to meet disapproval. She could never forget the Paris debacle, and her first Garcia audition. Even now she could see the Maestro shake his head slowly.

Again she had to call upon the forces of her strong will. Her voice was never sweeter as she sang her first aria in Philadelphia. In spite of themselves the audience relented, and clapped. After each song of surpassing richness and power, their applause increased in volume, until at the end Jenny was cheered with as much enthusiasm as at any concert so far in the New World.

One outstanding event, on her return to New York, was the concert attended by Daniel Webster — to Jenny, still the outstanding American of them all.

This concert was in Tripler Hall, built especially for the Jenny Lind visit. Mr. Webster and "his lady," as they called a wife in those days, were in the front row of the balcony, and everyone in the audience was aware of their mighty presence. Jenny sang through her usual arias, and Mr. Webster endured them. He was not musical, but the admiration between him and Jenny Lind was mutual. If she sang, he listened, no matter what.

Then someone heard Mrs. Webster say, "Why doesn't she sing some of her lovely native songs?" She knew her husband.

Word immediately flew backstage to Jenny, who

changed her next number and sang instead the famous Swedish "Echo Song." When she had finished she made one of her deep curtsies to the Websters, and Mr. Webster, in acknowledgment, stood up and bowed profoundly.

But in spite of all the honors and affection bestowed upon her, the healthy Swedish girl was tired. She had had two exhausting months with very little fresh air and almost no exercise. She had been subjected to untold indignities under the name of enthusiasm.

"Few people realize," she wrote home to her guardian, "how infinitely little the world with all its lustre means to me. Herring and potatoes, a clean wooden stool and wooden spoon to eat with, that would make me happy as a child . . ."

ON NOVEMBER 25, 1850, the Jenny Lind party started on its long countrywide tour that was to last until June, 1851. New York and Boston and Philadelphia were not America, even in 1850. Jenny was to see most of the United States east of the Mississippi — high-stepping, bouncing America, still in its gangling teens. She was to sleep in the best hotels the country had to offer; journey on new railroads just being built, on old horse-drawn stagecoaches bulging with passengers; sail on its finest steamboats; eat heartily and work hard. She and her musicians were blazing a trail that was later to be traveled by an ever-increasing number of artists from the Old World. Jenny Lind was a pioneer.

America in her day was a wild primitive land dotted with far-separated cities. Once she left the North she was to find herself centuries away from her native Europe. As she shivered in the badly heated, bumpy trains she would remember the snowy day when Hans Andersen met her in pretty Weimar, the luxurious sleigh rides under rich fur robes from the ducal palace. As she met the provincial people of America she would sometimes think of the musical elite whom she had known so well, the Schumanns, Mendelssohn of treasured memory, Meyerbeer. . . .

She had a little European circle of her own with her, it is true. But only Giovanni, of them all, lifted her out of the drabness of her worries. Josephine was her religious mentor, not one with whom she could laugh. Benedict was not in good health. Max, her boyish cousin, was far more interested in the New World than he was in her. But with Giovanni, she could walk and talk and remember. The past trailed along with them, and the present was more gracious when the lighthearted Italian was there. She was glad to have Giovanni nearby. Sometimes when his eyes looked into hers too earnestly, she was a little flustered; when his hand held hers too long, or too warmly. But she shook off the uneasiness, instead of facing it. She and Giovanni were old friends. Good friends. That was all.

The southbound party was enlarged by Mr. Barnum's daughter, Caroline, and a friend of hers, Mrs. Lyman from Bridgeport. Also in the retinue were Barnum's manager, Le Grand Smith, and twelve of the sixty-man orchestra used in New York. In each city the orchestra was to be supplemented by the use of local talent.

In Baltimore they stayed at a hotel called the Barnum, which Jenny later remembered as having the best water supply in all America. A storm was raging while they were there, and when Jenny stepped out onto the balcony to wave her greeting to the great crowds gathered below, the wind caught her shawl and blew it down into the mob. They at once fell upon it and tore it to pieces for souvenirs.

Washington, the next city, was surprisingly small for the capital of a nation. But Washington doffed its high hat to Jenny, bowed low, and spread the velvet cape for her feet.

"Such friendliness!" she told Josephine, after a visit to President Fillmore in the White House. "Such simplicity in this American court!"

Jenny's two Washington concerts were attended by the President and his family, every member of the Cabinet, most of the Congressmen, and the great Senators Thomas Hart Benton of Missouri and her much admired Daniel Webster (who seemed to get about almost as much as she!). The hall in which she sang was so new that the plaster on the walls was not yet dry, and the dignitaries had to sit on wooden benches. But no one cared, for Jenny never sang more sweetly.

One day Jenny and her party were invited to

Mount Vernon by Colonel Washington, a relative of the first President. They sailed along the Potomac, visited George Washington's tomb, and then Mt. Vernon itself where Colonel Washington's lady served them a dainty tea. It was one of the pleasantest of all Jenny's days in America.

As they were leaving, Mrs. Washington gave Jenny a book from the first President's library with his name inscribed in his own handwriting.

"What can I give them in return?" Jenny asked Mr. Barnum anxiously. She felt that she should not accept such a valuable gift.

The little watch which Queen Desideria had given her was always pinned on her breast — the watch that was to remind her when it was time to go back

home to Sweden. That might be a fitting gift. But she was superstitious. Perhaps if she gave it away she never *would* return!

Mr. Barnum told her she should not part with such a personal gift. By her presence she had done *them* a favor.

Still doubtful, but greatly relieved, Jenny pinned the watch back on.

The cities were getting smaller. The traveling was getting rougher.

From Washington to Richmond, Virginia, they had to go by steamboat and stagecoach. From Richmond to Wilmington, North Carolina, by rail.

Jenny looked forward to a novel experience. But little did she know how novel! Railroads in 1850 were in their infancy. The line from Richmond to Wilmington was still being built and its roadbed was not unlike a roller-coaster for shake-ups and sudden side shifts.

The whistle of the steam engine is now a memory of the past. But for a hundred years it was a message from the outside world to the American people living in distant villages and on lonesome farms. Many people still remember that long, shrill faraway whistle in the night. The engines had names and personalities. The trains had numbers. And people in small places watched for each scheduled stop. They worried when Number 4 was late. The engineer was a figure of romance, the ideal to small boys that the airplane pilot has now become.

Even the cars were different. Americans traveled sociably in those days. Each car was open from front door to back, with a wood-burning stove in the middle and plenty of spitoons.

Jenny and Barnum and their party traveled seventy-five miles on the new railroad to the little town of Weldon, where supper was provided for them at the hotel. Spiritually Weldon was one of their low points. The tired travelers had scarcely started eating when a hundred or more people filed silently into the dining room and took places among the tables and against the wall where they could best see Jenny Lind. Avidly but silently they watched her put her fork to her plate and raise it to her mouth.

Had they bought tickets? The incident was never explained, but Jenny could not bear the ordeal. She put her napkin to her mouth and hurried out, whether to be sick or to laugh has not been recorded.

The night train from Weldon to Wilmington, which they soon boarded, had narrow wooden shelves for beds.

This, thought Jenny, as she lay wide awake, *is the price of charity.*

EVEN BARNUM admits that the boat trip from Wilmington, North Carolina, to Charleston, South Carolina, was "exceptionally rough."

The S.S. *Gladiator* from Wilmington was due at Charleston at 11 A.M. This was the week before Christmas, and a dangerous gale was howling along the Atlantic Coast. Every ship on that storm-swept sea was in peril. (An SOS by radio was still many years in the future.)

By the following midnight the ship had not been heard from. All through the next day the people of Charleston watched fearfully, rain and wind beating on their faces as they stared out from the sea wall into the raging gray ocean.

By six that evening the storm had not abated, and they gave the ship up as lost. Word was telegraphed to the northern cities of the sinking of the *Gladiator* with its roster of famous passengers. The announcement appeared in heavy type in newspapers across the country.

It was indeed a fearful journey. While everyone on land was mourning its loss, the little ship was tossing like a cork on mountainous waves. Belletti and Benedict were hopelessly seasick. Barnum never once left his bunk. Jenny and Josephine were on their knees in prayer. "A kind Father controls us all," chanted Jenny. "Let His will be done!" added Josephine.

The ship finally reached Charleston two days late. But the wind had subsided, and in the early morning sunshine, the harbor and the city beyond were the picture of peace.

Charleston was a wealthy city flowering in the warmth and languor of the South. Its beautiful houses along the Battery were probably lovelier than any

the Europeans knew, and the gardens, even in December, were still green.

Every pleasant afternoon the promenade on the Battery was bright with the Charlestonian fashionables who strolled round and round, the ladies arm in arm, in their full skirts, velvet jackets, and lace-trimmed little bonnets; the gentlemen in tight light-colored trousers, bowing, smiling, passing the time of day in gallant true-southern style.

All through the South Jenny had seen slaves at work. It had been a shock when she first saw them in Maryland. But the vast number in Charleston amazed and horrified her. She sometimes went down to the river's edge, where she saw the Negroes arriv-

ing in small boats from plantations up the river, with
baskets, woven mats, and garden produce to sell. She
loved to watch the women, so erect, with bundles on
their heads, singing as they walked along the quay.
Was it like this in Africa? she wondered. But she
never ceased to shudder when she heard the drum-
beat that called the slaves to work in the morning.
(Later she was to meet Harriet Beecher Stowe, when
her book came out — the sad romantic *Uncle Tom's
Cabin*, which Jenny deeply admired.)

Christmas was approaching, and Christmas Eve
for Scandinavians was the greatest festival of the
year. That was why, three years before, Hans Andersen had so happily expected to spend it with Jenny
when they were both in Berlin. If Jenny now remembered, it would be with a twinge of conscience
that she had forgotten the poor Dane's existence.

What she best remembered, and what she would
remember every Christmas of her life, was Mendelssohn's present of three of his songs in his own handwriting, written especially for her! No matter where
she might be, the sudden sharp memory of Mendelssohn always brought her hand to her breast to quiet
the sudden pang. She would never be able to forget
the grace, the laughter, the happiness of their days
together.

In Charleston — so far from home — Jenny determined to make her own Swedish Christmas. She gave a surprise party and invited the whole troupe. They had a gay evening, eating and singing in German and Italian and English, and laughing at Barnum's Yankee jokes.

At midnight Jenny opened wide doors into the next room. There, gaily lighted, stood the Christmas tree which she had brought in secretly and trimmed. Under it was an alluring pile of packages with something for everybody.

For Barnum she had a statuette of Bacchus, god of wine — a good-natured gibe at his temperance.

"At least you must dance with me!" she cried, as the musicians began to tune up.

That was another thing Barnum could not do. "My education has been neglected!" he told her. Life in grim Connecticut had not included dance steps.

But she insisted, and because she was such a lovely dancer they somehow managed. Once was enough, however. After that she was willing enough to dance with the handsome Giovanni.

Although she gave only two concerts there, Jenny stayed ten days in Charleston, ten friendly peaceful days. A blessed respite.

A STILL GAYER VACATION awaited Jenny in sunny Cuba. But a black shadow hung on the horizon.

The party left Charleston January 2, 1851, and three days later arrived in the old Spanish city of Havana. Barnum as usual had thought of everything. As he had previously delivered a piano to the *Atlantic* when Jenny crossed to America, so now he had sent an agent from New York to find a house in Havana. He had even sent furniture, so that Jenny could step from the ship into a hospitable home.

The agent, however, took the easy way, and hired a few rooms in a hotel already half filled with guests.

Barnum was sorely disappointed. And Jenny could scarcely speak for anger. She refused to take off her bonnet. Without a word to anyone, not even to Josephine, she rushed from the house and was gone for four hours.

Jenny, the timid girl, who had always let her friends in Europe make the decisions, was once more proving that she was now a woman with a mind of her own. When she left in a rage, she picked up a *volante* (Cuban variation of a hackney coach) pulled by a thin old horse, spoke Italian to the driver, which he understood because it was so much like Spanish, and went house-hunting on her own.

Before sundown she had found what she wanted and rented it on the spot — a charming villa outside the walls of old Havana, with garden and court-yard, trees, bougainvillaea, hibiscus, and a driveway of waving palms. Flushed with triumph she returned and invited the whole party, including Barnum and Caroline and Mrs. Lyman to come and live with her.

She was a child again, but happier than she had been when really a child. She ran rather than walked, she played with the little Negro children, and teased Barnum — always a sure sign of good spirits.

Jenny loved Old World Havana, little knowing that Havana was weaving a plot for her destruction.

Barnum had inklings of trouble when they arrived. But he did not confide his worries to Jenny. The *Habaneros* were up in arms. They were unwilling to pay United States prices for concert tickets. They never had. Nonetheless they charged Barnum a huge sum for the Opera House, and in order not to lose money, he had to charge regular rates. He resisted all their protests, and the people of Havana — who had paid his prices — determined to get something for their money. They came to the concert to scorn, and, unlike the critical Philadelphians, they also came in anger.

On the night of the concert Jenny was still unaware of the gathering storm.

The audience did not applaud Benedict and the orchestra.

There was not a single handclap for Giovanni.

Then Jenny glided on stage in her white dress, with her smooth yellow hair. Her face, because of the Cuban sun, was browner and healthier than it had been at any time during her trip. With her hand in Belletti's, she came forward and stood in silence before the audience. A few people clapped when she reached the footlights. But the scanty applause was at once drowned out by hisses from all over the house.

Jenny could not believe it! There she was, willing and ready to sing. And they hated the very sight of her!

She was always tremulous at the first concert in a new city. It was part of her modest childlike appeal. This time she was also innocent of what lay ahead. But once she met hostility, the whole effect changed swiftly. In the face of the enemy she quickly gained complete self-mastery.

Up in the balcony Barnum saw it all. Still as a

statue she stood, coldly immovable. Only her eyes flashed. The fire within made her more beautiful than he had ever seen her. She was a gallant soul, his Jenny Lind!

Jenny knew that she must conquer these two thousand disgruntled people who for some reason wished her ill. They were gathered there to see her go down in confusion.

The orchestra started to play her aria. Not a sound came from the vast auditorium. Then she sang the opening notes of "Care Campagne" from *La Sonnambula*. She sang with power and tenderness and brilliance. Her voice poured forth its eloquence.

Barnum did not know what the words meant. He hung on the beauty of that voice, his heart near to breaking for her. At one point where the larklike notes rose effortlessly and died away in a long slow diminuendo, one person in the audience, unable to restrain himself, called "Brava!" At once the others shushed him. But only because they did not wish to miss a note.

When the song was done, the hall was silent for a long moment. Jenny turned to walk away, and then such applause burst forth as she had never received before, as if these hotheaded people felt a double appreciation because of their own unforgivable rudeness.

Five times Jenny was called back and stood before them, in her white gown, pure and untouched. Each time she made a deep curtsy, her head nearly bowed to the floor.

Barnum had watched her every move. His reputation was that of an astute businessman. But there were tears in his eyes — not in sorrow for his own cause, but for Jenny, and that moment of humiliation.

Now, after her resounding success, he rushed to the back of the stage just as she was running from her last curtain call. "God bless you, Jenny!" he cried.

She threw her arms around his neck. "Are you satisfied?" Tears were running down her cheeks too, tears of triumph.

"You've settled them."

Giovanni took her cold hand and held it in his own.

The contract called for twelve concerts, but Barnum refused to give more than four. The wealthy men of Havana, the Spanish Dons, begged him. They offered to put up $25,000. But Barnum said there was not money enough on the island to induce him to give more. Jenny gave her last concert for charity, as always, and the sad *Habaneros* knew it was the end.

Before they left Havana, Jenny had a visitor from Sweden, an old friend, the writer Fredrika Bremer.

Miss Bremer was touring the New World out of professional curiosity, and stayed with Jenny for a few days.

She at once asked Jenny to tell her about her fabulous success. But Jenny would not talk of concerts. No matter what the applause, what the remuneration, her heart was not in them. *She* wanted to talk of old friends and of Sweden.

Fredrika marveled at this strange absence of worldly interest. Here was probably the greatest singer the world had ever known, and she was apparently miserable in her profession. So they talked about the past. About the old days. With not a word about money or success or the vital present.

In spite of the good companionship, Fredrika found her friend sad. Jenny seemed to desire something that she had not found. Perhaps she wanted a home. She had never had one. Perhaps she wanted to be married, even though she had refused the three men who had wooed her. Her spirit was restless.

When Jenny and Mr. Barnum and the whole party left Havana, Miss Bremer sent Jenny a big bouquet of roses, and went down to the ship to see her off. The last view she had was of Jenny with her fair head buried in the roses, healthy and brown from her Cuban holiday, but infinitely sad.

NEW ORLEANS was a pretty sight as the ship bearing the musical party steamed in. The harbor was dotted with vessels from all over the world. The sun flashed a brilliant welcome.

Jenny felt reasonably content. One more chapter was finished, another about to start. The New World Tour had reached the halfway mark!

Then she saw the wharf — solid with people. "I can't face it, Mr. Barnum!" she cried. And she shrank back into the cabin.

Barnum patted her arm, as he always did when she grew difficult. "I'll fix it, Miss Lind. I'll fix it. Just give me a ten-minute start!"

The old practical joker had an idea. He asked his daughter Caroline to put on a thick veil and walk down the gangplank with her hand on his arm.

Most of the people of America knew by now what P. T. Barnum looked like, and in case they did not, the manager, Le Grand Smith, shouted from the ship's deck: "Make way, if you please, for Mr. Barnum and Miss Lind!"

The mob closed in on Barnum and Caroline, cheering, while Jenny sat quietly waiting in her cabin. When the dock was cleared, she and Josephine, escorted by Giovanni, went ashore with not a person the wiser. It may have been deceit, but Jenny's stiff standards were being tempered in the New World.

Jenny did not have to patronize the popular overcrowded Hotel St. Charles. Instead she was presented with a luxurious apartment on St. Peter's Street by a delightful, worldly-wise lady, Madam Montalba, who not only put the rooms at Jenny's disposal but supplied her with the best chef in the city. This meant the best in the country, because then as now, New Orleans was regarded as a mecca for gourmets. "Every meal a banquet!" Jenny wrote her guardian — Jenny, who preferred "herring and potatoes . . . and a wooden spoon"!

New Orleans was noted for its handsome Creoles — the people born there of French ancestry — and its irrepressible gaiety, as well as for good food. Every year at Mardi Gras the whole town danced in the streets for a week. Though this was not Mardi Gras, the visit of world-famous Jenny Lind was excuse enough for continuous celebration. A masked ball was given in her honor, and each of her concerts was a dazzling event.

Unlike most ladies of fashion, the ladies of New Orleans chose to dress alike, especially on holiday occasions. Their aim was not to create a new fashion but to enhance and beautify an old one. They wore white gowns of sheer gauze-like organdy, fluffy and full and airy, arms bare, neck cut low, and roses in the hair. The white powder they used on their faces added to the general effect of delicacy. Such nurtured femininity naturally called forth masculine gallantry, which made New Orleans gatherings the most attractively romantic in the world.

The first families of the city turned out for every Jenny Lind concert, and wealthy planters came in from their Mississippi River plantations, bringing their ladies and making a carnival of it, visiting relatives, giving big dinners, and dancing all night.

It was charming, but it was not Jenny Lind's cup of tea. This was a kind of lightheartedness of which her stricter northern code did not *quite* approve. Giovanni, however, was in his element. He liked everything about the French, and the Creoles, and the Italians — of whom there were many — and their cosmopolitan way of life. Sometimes he could persuade Jenny to wander with him about the old city, and they would stroll over to the very French Place d'Armes, the Cathedral of St. Louis, past dignified houses with narrow balconies of intricate wrought iron, to the French market redolent of fresh coffee, where they often stopped for refreshment.

Once they came unexpectedly upon the slave market, where a crowd of white men were gathered, shouting their bids. The auctioneer, in his wide hat, was calling them out, and the black men and women and children stood motionless beside him, waiting to be sold to the highest bidder. Jenny hurried away in horror. She tried to forget what she had seen. But the memory was implanted in her mind forever.

They remained a month in the old Creole city, and

gave twelve successful concerts, which brought Jenny alone $20,000!

Barnum was delighted, and his face was wreathed with smiles when he said good night to her on the eve of their departure from New Orleans. When Jenny did not return his smile, he charged it to tiredness. It was against human nature for her not to be happy now!

But little did he know.

"We are leaving this swampy city, threatened by floods from the Mississippi, and all kinds of fever," she wrote Judge Munthe that very night. "It won't be very amusing to travel for eight to ten days on the large river which looks as if it were only mud . . . But we expect to be back in New York by the end of April, and I hope to be finished with Barnum by the middle of June . . . I can't deny that I long to leave America!"

THE TRIP up the river turned out to be far less forbidding than Jenny had expected.

Mississippi steamboats were unique in the world. They scarcely looked like boats. Because the river was sometimes shallow, they had to have shallow draft, which made them ride *on* the water instead of *in* it. Since the hulls were shallow, the engines and boilers had to be on the main deck instead of below, as on most ships, and a second deck had to be added above to accommodate passengers. Eventually a third was built, giving the vessel an odd top-heavy look. The paddle boxes were bulky and big, the tall chimneys bellowed forth black smoke, and at night tongues of red flame.

The steamboat that Barnum had chosen was the handsomest on the river, the *Magnolia*. She was huge and towering and elegant beyond belief, with staterooms for more than 120 passengers, a barber shop, even a bathroom! The long cabin down through the center was a gorgeous tunnel separating the staterooms and serving as social hall and dining room for the passengers. Its ornamented ceilings were supported by great carved brackets, the windows were of stained glass, the bright large-patterned carpets were woven especially for it. There were imported chandeliers, oil paintings, heavy draperies, plush-covered furniture, a grand piano, and an enormous mirror at one end which added to the length and brilliance.

Many of the children had to sleep in the ladies' saloon because this was a crowded trip with not enough berths for all. Adventuring young lads, traveling light, slept out on deck with their heads on their knapsacks.

"I only hope that we won't be blown up in the air," Jenny had written Judge Munthe in her long, complaining New Orleans letter.

It is true that boiler explosions were frequent and disastrous on the river boats. The first steamboat had navigated the Mississippi in 1811, and now, only 40 years later, there was a record of 185 steamboats blown up with a loss of life of more than 1400 persons, many of them scalded to death!

But once aboard, amid the plush and the paint, who thought of danger?

As the ship plowed slowly north it passed big sugar plantations, and handsome pillared mansions up long avenues of live oaks. These were hot-weather houses, built a hundred years before air-conditioning. They had large rooms with ceilings sixteen feet high, with tall doors and wide windows always open to catch the breeze. They were hospitable homes with armies of servants, cooks, kitchen helpers, gardeners, yardmen, coachmen, grooms, dairymen, often a servant for each child. A guest, visiting one of these plantation houses, was taken on arrival into the big hall where a tall grandfather clock stood. The host stopped the clock. *Time stopped in this house while their guest was with them!*

They passed cotton plantations where Negroes were working in the fields, bandanas on their heads, baskets on their backs, and the ubiquitous white overseer in wide hat, standing over them. Here and there they would see a row of whitewashed one-story cabins. These were the slave villages.

All along the lower Mississippi, great fortunes were being made. The Civil War (coming ten years later) and the emancipation of slaves, would put an end to this prosperity, and the sumptuousness of plantation living would vanish for ever. But Jenny saw it at the height of its splendor.

Barnum planned that the passengers should not be bored. One day he arranged a concert in the ladies' saloon in which all the musicians, including

Belletti and Jenny, took part. Jenny, sitting casually at the piano, sang the old sweet songs that everybody knew — "Comin' Through the Rye," "The Last Rose of Summer," "John Anderson, My Jo." The air was damp and soft, and the constant plunging of the paddle wheel made a not unpleasant monotone of motion.

Another time, four of the crew danced a "breakdown on the hen coop," while two of the Negroes fiddled. Jenny loved that!

Barnum did card tricks and told anecdotes that kept the passengers in an uproar. Jenny thought they were funny the first time. But the charm soon wore off. Now when he took over, Jenny and Giovanni slipped out on deck, where the stars hung low.

Barnum arranged with the ship's captain for two stopovers, Natchez and Memphis, each long enough for a single concert. St. Louis was their objective.

(At Natchez, Jenny sang in a small Methodist chapel almost entirely filled with Negroes. Barnum thought it scarcely worthy of his Nightingale. But Jenny confided to Giovanni — who always understood — that never had Handel's "I Know That My Redeemer Liveth" been more appreciated.)

The Mississippi, swollen with spring floods, was adrift with floating trees and logs through which the *Magnolia* had to weave her way. These and hidden "snags" were, next to boiler explosions, the greatest menaces to Mississippi travel. To pilot through this floating forest took a practiced hand.

Indian canoes were a common sight, shooting their way in and out among the river boats, skillfully avoiding the tons of floating debris. They sometimes saw an Indian camp, and white men's villages made up of scattered log huts which one day would be a town. The people in these primitive settlements were friendly, and waved and shouted greetings. The Indians only stared.

(St. Louis and Nashville, Louisville and Cincinnati)

18

THE PLANTERS HOTEL in St. Louis was a magnificent hostelry, with long windows, colonnades, and high wide steps. As Jenny and her party drove up, on the night of their arrival, it was aglow with light.

St. Louis itself was aglow for Jenny. This was a vigorous fast-growing city of 77,000 — one of the gateways to the West, and imbued with the spirit of adventure. Every day covered wagons could be seen on the riverbank preparing for the long trek across the plains. Strangers were constantly moving through.

The only unchanging part of the city was the old French quarter, a labyrinth of narrow streets lined with tall houses leaning precariously against each other. They had galleries round the upper stories, and outside steep stairways that went up from ground to roof. This of course charmed Giovanni and Benedict. Here they strolled, patronized the little French barber shop, already famous, and listened to the talk of bearded westerners. A rough lot, they reported to Jenny and Josephine, but genial.

St. Louis was a racing town, and in one race four of the horses entered were: Barnum, Jenny Lind, Belletti, and Benedict. (Benedict won!)

Jenny sang five concerts, the last her seventieth in America. Anything she wished to sing was received with warm enthusiasm by the eager unspoiled audiences.

The party had now left the elegant *Magnolia*, and for the next step of the journey took a small overcrowded steamboat to Nashville — Nashville-on-the-Cumberland, in the bluegrass country of Tennessee.

Spring had come to cast its spell upon them.

As he so often did, Giovanni asked Jenny to walk with him. It was their last day in Nashville, and they strolled along the riverbank. The fragrance of apple blossoms and the songs of birds were blended in the soft, warm air. April stirred strange yearnings. Giovanni was restless and Jenny was silent. A vague discontent with the commonplace world possessed them.

For the first time Jenny heard the warbling of the mockingbird, from the branch of a nearby tree. Its unrehearsed improvised beauty made her inexplicably sad.

When Giovanni saw a tear roll down her cheek, he

had an impulse to take her in his arms, to protect her against all mysterious unhappiness — against crude Barnum or noisy crowds or dark, shadowy memories. Here they were, he and Jenny, in the wilderness, in the very center of the New World! He stood silent before her, but Jenny could read, as in an open book, that he loved her.

Many times she and Giovanni had walked companionably through the countryside. Often she had found him looking at her strangely, but she had laughed and talked, and somehow broken the spell.

This was different, however. She could feel the intensity of this deeper, stronger mood. But she turned her head away, and with an almost imperceptible motion of the hand, rejected him. In silence they walked back toward the city. The good companionship was threatened. What lay ahead, neither tried to guess.

Jenny took the first step. She announced that evening that she and Josephine, instead of continuing by steamboat with the rest of them, would go overland, and meet them at Louisville. They would visit famous Mammoth Cave. They would go by stagecoach — exchange the dangers of "blowing up" for "breaking down." She tried to sound nonchalant.

As she gave her ultimatum, she gazed straight at Barnum. But he remained silent. There was nothing he could say, for the Nightingale's feathers must not be ruffled. But "Never a quiet moment!" he no doubt thought to himself.

Her eyes rested for only a moment on Giovanni.

The rain came down in torrents as the two women faced northward. The muddy road was all but impassable. Passengers in the coach were thrown against each other, and the luggage, tied on top, slid and slipped and got soaking wet. This was the most rugged overland passage of the entire tour. Yet Jenny enjoyed it. Whenever they stopped to change horses, they found odd characters standing idly about —

mountain men, tall and lanky. Children were everywhere, pigs in abundance. But at last she was anony-
mous. No one here had ever heard tell of Jenny Lind!

Mammoth Cave was also worth the journey. It
was tremendous and forbidding: level upon level of
gruesome chambers connected by dark narrow passages; the Green River flowing mysteriously below;
blind fish — bats — insects. It was exciting and fearful. Jenny was glad she had seen it, but not sorry
when they stepped once more into the clean air of
God's outdoors.

Louisville was a welcome sight to the two tired,
dirty travelers, and Barnum and the others greeted
them as though they had been separated for months.
Jenny and Giovanni were never alone, but behaved

among the others as naturally as possible.

For the first time in America Jenny did not appear in white, probably because stagecoach travel had been too much for her white dress. Instead she wore pink — a pink gown trimmed with fringe, pink flowers, fresh from the garden, in her hair, and spick-and-span white gloves. She looked charming. When everyone complimented her, she smiled shyly at Giovanni.

There was another novelty. Signor Salvi, an Italian tenor whom Barnum engaged while in Havana, joined them here, and bowed low to Miss Lind. Giovanni at first regarded his compatriot with suspicion, but before long they became good friends. Salvi sang at the three concerts with great success.

From Louisville they sailed up the Ohio to Cincinnati on the *Ben Franklin*, almost as luxurious a boat as the *Magnolia*. Once more they were a united family and happy to be together.

When they reached Cincinnati it was six o'clock in the morning and the dock was already black with people waiting for Jenny Lind.

This time Jenny looked bitterly at Barnum. "I *won't* face it!" She was no longer piteous. She was indignant.

Barnum tried a new ruse. He couldn't repeat the New Orleans arrival stunt because the newspapers all over the country had picked up the story. (Jenny Lind was still Big News.) Instead, he took Jenny by the arm, and had her wear a thick veil. Again Le Grand Smith was instructed to stand on deck, only this time he shouted: "No go, Barnum! You can't pass your daughter off as Jenny Lind *this* time!"

The crowd bellowed. "You may fool the New Orleans folk, but you can't come it over the Buckeyes!" They made way for Barnum and the lady, and awaited the real thing. It was a good half-hour before they realized that Barnum had fooled *them* too.

When Charles Dickens visited Cincinnati in 1842 it had 50,000 inhabitants. Now, nine years later, it had 115,436! Many of the new settlers were Germans and with them had come a surge of interest in music and art.

Our musicians were delighted to be able again to speak the language they all loved. Especially Jenny. For the moment, she felt herself back in a neat little German provincial city, and her heart beat fast with memories.

Here she sang German music, to audiences that were deeply appreciative. Indeed, for many of them the concerts were also nostalgic with Old World memories, of cities and high-steepled churches, and a *Gewandhaus* ringing with beautiful sound. . . .

(Wheeling, Pittsburgh, the Mountains)

19

THE BANKS of the Ohio were still covered with stretches of unbroken forest. Sometimes, around a bend, the boat passengers would see smoke rising from a settlement. Here men had made clearings and built log cabins. These were settling folk, not adventurers bound for California gold. Many of these clusters of log cabins would soon be towns, and — when railroads came — they would become thriving industrial cities.

It was a three-day trip from Cincinnati to Pittsburgh, which they interrupted at Wheeling long enough to give one concert. Wheeling itself was a busy city making nails and glass and "stogies," those long, thin, cheap cigars that nearly sickened the musicians. There were many nationalities living here, Scotch, Irish, some German, mostly simple working people for whom Jenny sang the old folk songs. Her picture was widely sold, and few were the family albums that did not treasure a portrait of the Nightingale with her smooth hair over the ears and her low-necked dress.

Pittsburgh was a nightmare — a smoky city built high over the Allegheny River, a city of clanking hammers and roaring furnaces, and coal miners. Nothing quite so calamitous had happened since the night of the Fitchburg Depot. The first concert was scheduled for a Friday, which was pay day for the miners. They came in from the mines in a solid body, to collect their money and to make a night of it. Many were drunk before sundown, and all of them, released from a week underground, were wildly boisterous.

They filled the streets around the hall where the Jenny Lind concert was going on, shouting and jeering. Some were singing maudlin songs and others who tried to quiet them, were almost as noisy. Stones began to fly.

Indoors Jenny went through her program, but few in the hall could hear her for the stampede outside. When the concert was over none of the performers dared leave the hall and face the mob. They put out the lights and sat in darkness, hoping that the miners would give up and drift away. But the miners were there to stay. Hour after hour, the musicians sat huddled together, and the drunken rioters milled and shouted.

Finally someone found a back door of the theater

which opened on a dark, evil-smelling alley. Jenny was led out this way, and at a very late hour, reached the hotel.

She could not leave the city soon enough! The second concert was abandoned, and early the next morning, after a sleepless night, the party left Pittsburgh forever.

Their way lay through the Allegheny Mountains, bold and striking, and unbelievably rough going. Even though they were headed for the Atlantic seaboard, civilization had never seemed farther away.

It had been an unforgettable trip in terms of scenic splendor, magnificent mountains and rushing rivers. But it was long and tiring. From the town of York they went by train back to Baltimore, thus completing the circle.

This was the end of the Linderama.

It was also almost the end of the journey of Barnum and Jenny Lind. They had traveled together 4000 miles, and (after the next group of eastern appearances) Jenny would have sung ninety-three concerts.

20

"You have *no idea how tired of it all I am!*" Jenny wrote to her guardian.

"*I had become weary,*" wrote Barnum in his journal. "*. . . I desired tranquillity.*"

Their emotions were frayed, and they were about ready to get on each other's nerves. But, let it be said to P. T. Barnum's lasting credit, he and Jenny Lind remained friends to the end. They parted, but not in anger.

For an easygoing man, as Barnum on the surface seemed to be — "smooth" to the point of oiliness as his enemies would have it — he was sensitive to the currents that ebbed about him. As soon as the party was again in the East he realized that adverse influ-

ences were working on Jenny against him. It might be Max Hjortzberg, who had always been something of a troublemaker, or it might have been her dignified counselor, Mr. Maunsell Field. More likely it was just strain: "... how tired of it all I am!" He sensed the direction in which her mood was carrying her, and as usual it was he who took the first step.

It was in the National Theatre in Philadelphia where Jenny had just sung her ninety-third concert in America. A slight stable odor hung in the air, reminder of the circus troupe that had performed there the night before. Jenny sniffed disdainfully.

Barnum came into her dressing room, waved Max out, and addressed himself to her. "Miss Lind, I do not wish to stand in your way ..." He told her that although their contract specified 100 concerts, he would release her from the next seven if she so wished. All he wanted was her happiness. His friendly smile confirmed his good will.

Jenny, who in all their time together had never learned to appreciate Barnum's quick perceptiveness, was surprised. But she accepted the arrangement on the spot, and agreed to pay him a token amount for the remaining concerts. Her relief was obvious.

To be sure, nobody was hurt. Jenny had already earned over $150,000 in nine months, and Mr. Barnum was financially well content. "Iranistan" beckoned. Its splendors might be rich and exotic, but its demands on him were refreshingly simple.

The parting between Jenny and Giovanni was not so easy.

As Julius Benedict had to return to London at the end of May, Jenny, now her own manager, was obliged to find a new accompanist. Her mind at once darted to the young man she had known in Germany, the pupil of Mendelssohn, Otto Goldschmidt. He had been with her in Lübeck just before she decided to make the American tour. He was part of the past.

It was he who had persuaded her to sing Mendelssohn's songs once more. She had sung them and he had played her accompaniment. His whole personality was suffused with the glow of Mendelssohn. . . .

Otto Goldschmidt came to America as soon as he received Jenny's call. His memories too were alive and warm.

It was when Giovanni saw Jenny and Otto together that he realized the final collapse of his hopes. Jenny had found her own at last. It was as if all this time she had been waiting, and now he had come! Her face lighted when this serious young German entered the room. Her eyes at once found his.

Giovanni had been close to Jenny too long and through too many experiences, not to understand that a deep change was taking place behind that seemingly placid brow. She had taken him for granted — Giovanni the lighthearted and, as she probably thought, the light-minded. It was now Otto with whom she walked and talked and discussed, no doubt, the romantic past and the uncertain future. She was kind to Giovanni — when she remembered him!

Giovanni tried to sing, but his heart was not in it. When he appeared for a concert his eyes were red — whether from tears or from sleepless nights, one could not tell. But Jenny barely noticed. As she had been a "sister" to Hans Christian Andersen, so she had been only a "good companion" to Giovanni Belletti. Now she was scarcely that.

"I must go!" he finally told her — only that. But his sad eyes revealed the depth of his feeling.

For a moment Jenny was startled into a deeper realization. Tremulously she put her hand on his arm and urged him to stay.

It was too late. Giovanni went back to Europe. Eventually he returned to Italy. He continued to sing, but lived a lonely life, and never married.

Jenny, who now arranged her own affairs, had Signor Salvi take Belletti's place on the program, while Otto Goldschmidt accompanied her in all her concerts.

"Next to Mendelssohn," she wrote her guardian,

"he is the most musical man I have ever known. When he accompanies me it is as if I accompanied myself."

His appeal extended far beyond music. "He is the first person," she wrote, "that I feel — in all ways before God — I am created for. He can fulfill all the needs of my soul! And I in turn can make him happy. *But he is so young!* If I should leave him no other person could take my place — of that I am sure. And my own life would be hopeless. But the age difference! The age!" It was a long letter, written with passion. "Only to you, dear Guardian, not even to Josephine, have I told all this! Send me some soothing words — some advice!"

He is so young. That was the only obstacle that Jenny saw in the blissful future that so suddenly opened up ahead. Otto was seven years younger than she. But he was just as much in love. From the first time he had heard her, in Leipzig, when he was seventeen, he had worshiped the Nightingale from afar. Now that he knew Jenny Lind, the warmhearted young woman, shy and uncertain, for all her worldly success, he loved her even more. He loved her tenderly, and protectively.

In the young German, Jenny saw the answer to her dream. Her cool northern temperament responded to his gravity and goodness. Neither gaiety nor fun satisfied her long. She had had her fill of fame. What she wanted now was safety, security, and quiet peacefulness — blessings which her dramatic and exciting life had denied her. Deep in her heart she knew that Otto Goldschmidt was offering something she had craved since she was four years old — the golden haven of a home.

Jenny and Otto were married in Boston on February 5, 1852, at the home of Mr. and Mrs. Gray Ward, in Louisburg Square. It was a small wedding. The Honorable Edward Everett was present, Jenny's elderly admirer who had taken her out to Harvard on the night of the meteor; the Swedish Consul; and Mr. and Mrs. Ward. The Wards gave Jenny a gold locket containing daguerreotypes of the two Americans she most admired, George Washington and Daniel Webster. She wore it for the rest of her life.

The bride and groom went to Northampton for their honeymoon and stayed for three long happy months. They climbed Mount Tom and visited Paradise Lake, to which Jenny gave its name. This was many years before Smith College had peopled Northampton with girls.

Jenny's mother died while Jenny was in America, and Judge Munthe followed her harsh body to the grave. Jenny's father at once began begging for more funds. Every letter to Jenny and to Judge Munthe asked for money. But Jenny at last had a protective hand folded over her own. Otto took up her troubles, financial as well as personal, and left both Jenny and her dear guardian carefree and easy of mind.

There were forty more Jenny Lind concerts in America, though none was so successful as the concerts given under Barnum's inspired management.

The last concert, like the first, was sung at Castle Garden. It was May 24, and raining hard. Barnum came into her dressing room to say goodbye. His face was again wreathed in smiles. He was already deep in new shows, new tours, new freaks for his Museum. Jenny too was professionally satisfied. "I am thankful to say," she told him, "that I have all the money which I shall ever need!"

Jenny left our shores on the same ship, the *Atlantic*, on which she had come. In spite of the fact that it was raining and that the ship sailed at one o'clock in the morning, several hundred people gathered at the dock to see her off, among them three hundred of the faithful New York Fire Department, in scarlet shirts and again carrying torches.

This is the end of the story of Jenny Lind in America.

Jenny and Otto were contentedly, harmoniously, energetically happy together for the rest of their lives. They made their home in England on the edge of Wimbledon Common, where Jenny had first heard the nightingales sing. They had three children, and a warm, cozy, family life. Jenny's oldest daughter once described them all grouped around the old harmonium on Christmas Eve, singing "Good King

Wenceslas," to their mother Jenny's accompaniment. This was the childhood she herself had missed.

The Goldschmidts were close friends of Queen Victoria and the Prince Consort. In fact the English used to call Otto the Prince Consort of Music. Their intimates were aristocrats, and working people, and artists. They knew no class distinctions. "Who's coming for dinner tonight?" the same daughter once asked Jenny. "Oh, the King of Sweden and Mr. Smithers," Jenny answered, without a trace of self-consciousness. Mr. Smithers was the local organist.

America had turned her against public life. She was through with publicity and applause and crowds. She sang less and less as the years went by, but assisted Otto in his musical teaching, and later joined the faculty of the Royal Conservatory of Music. She personally trained the sopranos for the first performance in England of Bach's great *Mass in B Minor* given in 1876, under Goldschmidt's direction. She could not have been more content.

On the last morning of Jenny's life, in the pretty Goldschmidt home in the Malvern Hills, a ray of sun came in and touched the face of the dying woman. Her daughter and her husband were with her, and they heard the faint voice sing the opening bars of Robert Schumann's "An den Sonnenschein." The

Nightingale was remembering the past.

In the Poets' Corner of Westminster Abbey, under the statue of Handel, is a plaque of Jenny's head in profile. It is of pure white marble, and around it are the words: "I Know That My Redeemer Liveth."

INDEX